AF254553

The Science of Charisma:
174 Small Behavioral Tweaks For Charm, Likability, and Rapport (Backed By Research)

By Patrick King
Social Interaction and Conversation Coach at
www.PatrickKingConsulting.com

Table of Contents

Introduction: The Science of Charisma in Real Life

Most conversations don't blow up. They just go flat with that weird drop in energy both people feel and politely ignore.

You know the feeling: a reply comes a little too fast, a joke almost lands, or the whole vibe shifts for no obvious reason. You walk away thinking, "Yeah, that was fine," and technically it was, but it didn't click, it didn't stick, and it definitely didn't move the relationship forward.

This book is for that exact space. The pause after your joke where you wonder if it worked, the text you rewrote five times and somehow made less natural each round, the meeting where you meant to be direct and sounded sharp, the dinner where everyone talked and smiled and still went home not one inch closer. These moments look small, but they quietly run a huge percentage of our social lives.

So what does the title mean? When I say *The Science of Charisma*, I'm talking repeated psychological patterns that have been studied again and again: certain moves consistently make people feel safe, seen, and interested, while other moves make people pull back, even when your intentions are good. Everything in this book is supported by research on how to be more charming, attractive, and charismatic.

The good news: patterns can be practiced and even mastered.

Conversation is a skill, not a personality lottery, and it's built from tiny choices: where your attention goes, how fast you respond, how much room you give, what question you ask next, and whether your tone feels rushed or grounded. Those choices look small, but they change everything. One clean follow-up can turn polite small talk into real momentum, and one well-timed pause can stop a defensiveness spiral before it starts.

That's the science in this book: small moves, predictable social effects, repeated until they feel natural. That's also why the book is built as 174 compact tips.

Each tip is designed for real life, not perfect conditions. You can use them in group chats, on dates, in meetings, at family dinners, in text threads, and in those random in-between moments where you suddenly realize, oh, this interaction matters. The goal isn't to perform charisma; it's to make connection easier.

You'll see research throughout, but this isn't a theory-only book. You can read one tip and use it the same day, or move through the whole thing gradually and let the reps compound. Both approaches work. Just don't confuse understanding with progress, because the shift comes from practice.

As you start, keep one rule in mind: direction over perfection.

You'll miss cues, overtalk one day and under-talk the next, and try new moves that feel awkward at first. That's normal. What matters is staying curious, keeping what works, dropping what doesn't, and returning to the moves that consistently make your conversations warmer, clearer, and more honest.

If this book works the way it should, two things happen: your conversations feel lighter and less effortful, and the people around you feel more at ease opening up. That combination quietly changes friendships, dating, teamwork, leadership, and family dynamics over time.

You don't need a new personality. You need better reps. Let's begin.

How to Use This Book

This book works best when you treat it like a training plan, not a one-time read.

Here is the simplest way to use it:
1. Pick one tip per day.
2. Try it once in a real conversation.
3. Write one line after: what changed, what did not, what to tweak.
4. Repeat for seven days before adding more.

Chapter 1: The Spotlight Is in Your Head

You know that moment when you trip over absolutely nothing in public and instantly assume the entire planet saw you? Yeah, psychologists have a name for that. In 2000, Thomas Gilovich and his colleagues ran a delightfully humbling study where they had participants wear an embarrassing Barry Manilow T-shirt, then guess how many people noticed. The wearers were convinced everyone clocked it. In reality, only a small fraction did.

Turns out, no one's paying as much attention to you as… you. Our brains love to believe we're the main attraction, but most folks are too busy worrying about their own imaginary audience to track your every misstep. This little ego bruise is actually a relief.

When you drop the idea that the world's watching, you can relax. You can show up to conversations without analyzing your facial expressions like you're auditioning for a crime drama. You can make decisions without looping through a highlight reel of possible embarrassments. The spotlight effect isn't a character flaw. It's just a quirk of human psychology that, once seen clearly, lets you breathe easier and get on with living.

Tip 1: Show Up Imperfectly

The fastest way to shrink that imaginary spotlight? Do something small and mildly awkward on purpose. Ask a "dumb" question in a meeting. Wear the shirt you're not sure is cool. Stumble through the first five minutes of a new hobby class. Treat these moments like reps at the psychological gym. Each time you survive a tiny embarrassment, you teach your brain that nothing catastrophic follows. People rarely notice, and if they do, it's forgotten faster than last week's leftovers. A simple daily rep: once a day, let yourself be imperfect in public. Not sloppy, just human. Speak up before your sentence is perfectly polished. Make a decision without running it by your imaginary critics.

The aim isn't to chase embarrassment. It's to build tolerance for visibility so your life stops orbiting around other people's nonexistent scrutiny.

Tip 2: Shift Your Attention Outward

When your brain's screaming "everyone's watching me," it's usually because your attention is turned inward, dissecting every micro-movement like a forensic scientist. Flip that spotlight around. Get curious about whoever's in front of you. What's their energy like? What's something you can appreciate about them? How can you make this interaction easier for both of you? Shifting from self-monitoring to other-awareness immediately softens self-consciousness. Give yourself one job in the next conversation: listen for one interesting detail you can ask a follow-up question about. That's it. Directing your attention outward does two things. First, it quiets your inner narrator. Second, it makes you a better conversational partner.

Ironically, the more you focus on others, the more confident and natural you feel. And that's when the real magic happens: you stop performing and you actually show up.

Chapter 2: Talk Less, Connect More

Picture two people talking. One takes most of the airtime. The other nods and waits for a turn. We've all been both.

A practical rule of thumb is to talk about 30 percent of the time and listen about 70 percent. Not because silence is virtuous or because you should shrink yourself, but because people feel connected when they feel heard. And most people just aren't heard enough.

When you give someone space to speak, you send a clear signal that they matter. You're saying, "I care about your world," without announcing it. Think of it as conversational hospitality. You make room for someone else to exist fully in your presence. That's rare, and memorable.

Without intention, many conversations become one-person podcasts. This chapter is how you dodge that.

Tip 3: Be a Noticer

Sometimes someone says, "It's fine," and everything in their tone says the opposite. That micro-mismatch is the signal most people miss because they're already preparing their reply. Stay with that moment instead of rushing past it.

This isn't about trying to decode every word like a detective. Just catch one thing that feels loaded: a weird pause, a repeated phrase, a sudden laugh that doesn't match the topic. Then ask one plain follow-up: "Wait, what part of that bothered you?" or "You paused there. What happened?" That's it. One detail. One question. A single clean follow-up often does more than five clever comments. You don't need to be the most interesting person in the room. You just need to be the one who actually noticed.

Tip 4: Speak With an Actual Point

Talking less doesn't mean disappearing into polite fog. It means your words do more work. Before you jump in, run a tiny filter: am I adding connection, clarity, or a little lift to the room? If yes, go for it. If not, let it die quietly in your brain where it belongs. The practical move is to keep your share to two or three sentences, then pass the ball back. "That reminds me of something similar, how'd it play out for you?" You stay present without turning the conversation into a solo show. Aim for precision, not silence for its own sake: say the part that helps, then hand the ball back while the energy is still alive.

Run a low-stakes rep today and watch the next ten seconds. If they visibly soften, the move is working.

Chapter 3: Match, Don't Mimic

In 1999, psychologists Tanya Chartrand and John Bargh ran a study that still gets name-dropped in communication workshops like it's a backstage pass to human connection. They found that people naturally and unconsciously mirror each other's posture, tone, and pacing. When this happens, trust and likability quietly rise. They called it the chameleon effect. Not the creepy lizard-copying kind, but the gentle, barely noticeable syncing humans do when they feel comfortable. The key is subtlety. This isn't about parroting someone like you're auditioning for a funhouse mirror. Too much imitation feels weird fast. What works is tiny alignment. You lean in slightly when they do. You slow your pace if they talk slowly.

You soften your tone when they soften theirs. Done well, it creates that easy, warm sense of "I get you." It's one of those rare social tools that helps both people relax. And once you understand it, conversations start feeling less like performance art and more like two humans navigating the same rhythm.

Tip 5: Tune Into Their Rhythm

Many people think mirroring is about copying movement, but the real magic happens when you match someone's emotional tempo. If they're enthusiastic, you let yourself meet that energy. If they're thoughtful and quiet, you dial it back. It's not about shapeshifting. You're respecting their internal pace. This tells their nervous system, "You're safe here," which is basically the secret handshake of rapport.

During your next interaction, pay attention to one thing only: pace. Are they talking quickly or slowly? Do they pause before answering? Try adjusting your tempo by just ten percent in their direction. Not a full send, just a nudge. You'll notice the conversation feels smoother, like you both caught the same wave.

With practice, this tiny calibration trains you to engage with people where they already are, which is the most generous social skill you can build.

Tip 6: Reflect the Meaning

Mirroring doesn't have to be physical. You can mirror values, intentions, or emotional undercurrents. If someone shares a frustration, you don't need to cross your arms because they did. You can mirror the meaning by acknowledging the experience: "That sounds rough." If they're proud of something, match the lift in their tone with genuine enthusiasm. You're reflecting the emotional truth, not copying their posture like you're following a choreography tutorial. What you can do: practice reflective listening in your next conversation. After they speak, give a short sentence that mirrors the emotional point.

Something like, "You seem really excited about that," or "Sounds like that took a lot of patience." This kind of mirroring builds trust faster than matching body angles ever will. People feel seen instead of studied. And that's the whole point of rapport. This isn't about trying to blend in. You're trying to meet someone in a shared moment where connection stops being effort and starts being natural.

Chapter 4: Build on What They Say

Back in 1979, improv legend Keith Johnstone put language to something humans have been doing since we first sat around fires telling stories. "Yes, and" is the golden rule of improv: accept whatever's offered, then build on it. No shutting ideas down. No pretending you're above the moment. No playing conversational goalie and blocking every shot. It's a deceptively simple mindset that transforms interactions from low-energy ping-pong into something that feels collaborative and alive.

In regular life, "yes, and" doesn't mean agreeing with everything like a hostage negotiator or pretending everything's brilliant. It means meeting what someone says with openness first. When someone shares an idea or story, you meet it with curiosity instead of critique.

You add something that moves the conversation forward instead of sideways. People relax around you because they sense you're not there to win. You're there to connect. That tiny shift turns conversations into shared adventures rather than verbal obstacle courses. And honestly, most of us could use more connection and fewer roadblocks.

Tip 7: Catch It Before You Correct It

The "yeah, but" reflex feels smart when it leaves your mouth. It usually lands like rejection. Even if your point is valid, people hear the "but" as: your thing is wrong, here's mine.

Try flipping the order. Start with connection, then add your view. "Yeah, I get why you'd do that, and I think we could tighten one part." Same idea, different emotional impact. It's not about fake-agreeing. You're just not slamming the door before you walk through it. Try it once today in a real conversation. Just once. Catch one "but," swap it to "and," and keep moving. You'll feel the temperature drop in real time.

Treat this like a habit you rehearse, not a trick you deploy. Repetition is what makes it natural.

Tip 8: Add Something That Moves the Story Forward

Most conversations die from polite agreement. "Nice." "Totally." "Makes sense." None of that is wrong, but none of it adds oxygen. To create momentum, respond in a way that gives the other person something to do next.

A good rule is: add one step. Ask what made them choose that route. Pull out one detail and get curious about it. Offer a short parallel and hand it back. You are not trying to impress them with your own story arc. You are extending theirs.

To build the habit, today in one real conversation: after they finish a point, make one additive move before switching topics. One follow-up question or one specific reaction is enough.

After a few reps, your presence changes. People feel that talking to you goes somewhere instead of looping in social autopilot. That feeling is a huge part of likability.

Chapter 5: Ask for a Small Favor

Benjamin Franklin, professional statesman and part-time social ninja, once pulled off a curious psychological trick. Instead of trying to win over a rival with charm, he asked the guy for a small favor. Shockingly, it worked. A couple centuries later, in 1969, researchers Jecker and Landy tested this odd little move. They found that when people do you a favor, they subconsciously rewrite the story to make it feel logical. "I helped them, so I must like them." Our brains hate loose ends, so we stitch them together into affinity. This flips the usual script. Most of us bend over backwards doing favors to earn goodwill, but Franklin's insight shows the reverse can be just as powerful.

Asking for a tiny bit of help doesn't make you needy. It makes the other person invested. It cracks open a door to rapport because we like feeling useful. And when someone lets us help them, we feel trusted. That's bonding fuel. Keep the request small, genuine, and human, and you'll be surprised by how quickly warmth appears.

Tip 9: Invite Help

We're taught that independence is noble and asking for help is a burden. Turns out, refusing help is often what blocks connection. When you ask for something small, you're not taking from someone. You're inviting them into your world. You're saying, "I trust you with this little piece of my life." People feel honored when they can contribute. And that sense of usefulness is its own reward. This week, pick a low-stakes favor. Ask a coworker to proofread two sentences. Ask a friend for a podcast recommendation.

Ask a neighbor if they know a good local spot for something. Keep it bite-sized. Afterward, offer a sincere thank-you and nothing more. No overpaying, no dramatic praise.

Let the psychological magic do its thing. The aim is to let people feel valued, not obligated. You'll notice conversations get easier, smiles get warmer, and the social distance shrinks.

Tip 10: Build a Generosity Loop

Once someone has done you a favor, don't rush to even the score. Reciprocity is good, but too-fast repayment shuts the loop. Instead, stay open to letting the relationship deepen. When the time naturally comes, offer something back that aligns with who you are. Not a grand gesture, just a thoughtful one. This builds a gentle rhythm: they help you, you help them, the connection roots itself. On your next rep: after someone helps you, pay attention to opportunities—not obligations—to support them. Maybe you introduce them to someone useful. Maybe you remember a detail they shared and check in later. Maybe you just show up with curiosity and presence.

The aim is a slow, steady exchange that feels human rather than transactional.

When you nurture this loop, friendships grow, collaborations get easier, and people start seeing you as someone they want in their corner. That's the real win Franklin stumbled onto.

One small behavior makes this easier: pause before you ask, and pause again after you ask. MIT researcher Alex Pentland's work on conversational rhythm suggests a similar pattern. People who aren't rushing tend to come off calmer and more credible.

That one-breath pause keeps your request from sounding grabby. It also gives the other person room to respond without pressure.

Tip 11: Add a Micro-Pause

Fast replies are overrated. Half the time they're not clarity, they're adrenaline.

Try a tiny pause before you ask, and again before you answer. One breath. Not a dramatic silence. Just enough space to keep your mouth from outrunning your intention.

Use it in low-stakes asks first: "Could you look at this sentence?" "Do you have a recommendation?" Then use the same pause in higher-stakes moments. It cuts down accidental sharpness, makes your tone steadier, and helps the other person feel invited instead of cornered.

If it feels a little awkward at first, that's expected. Keep the rep small and real; smoothness comes from repetition.

Chapter 6: Compliment What They Choose

Humans are hilariously easy to connect with. According to a 2012 study by Holmes, Miller, and Lerner at the University of Kansas, you just need... a compliment.

A sincere one. Not the plastic kind wrapped in awkwardness, but the real deal that makes someone feel like you actually noticed something meaningful about them. Their findings suggest that genuine compliments can trigger fast social bonding. It's like emotional Velcro. A few well-aimed words and suddenly two strangers become people who actually like each other.

The best part? Compliments that focus on effort or character land way harder than the "nice shirt" variety. When you acknowledge someone's kindness, consistency, or grit, you're shining a light on something they chose, something they earned.

People don't just feel flattered. They feel seen. And when someone feels seen, they warm up in ways that no algorithm can measure. Your likability rises, your interactions soften, and conversations start feeling less like transactions and more like connection. Not bad for a sentence you can deliver in under five seconds.

Tip 12: Compliment Someone's Choices, Not DNA

If you'd like your compliments to carry emotional weight, aim for traits people have built, not ones they were born with. Anyone can be told they have nice eyes. But telling someone you admire how patient they were in a stressful meeting? That's gold. It validates their behavior and encourages more of it. Once a day, look for a moment where someone's effort or character made something better. Then call it out. It doesn't need to be poetic. "I noticed how thoughtful you were with that customer" works fine. The magic is in the noticing. You'll be stunned by how quickly people relax around you. You go from background character to someone they trust.

And all because you took five seconds to reflect something good back to them.

Tip 13: Make It Specific Enough to Be Real

Generic praise is like decaf coffee. Technically it's the thing, but it doesn't do much. A specific compliment, though, is a mini spotlight that says, "I'm actually paying attention." When you tell someone exactly what they did that impressed you, they internalize it differently. It becomes feedback, affirmation, and encouragement all at once. When you decide to compliment someone, add one concrete detail. Instead of "Great job," try "I loved how clearly you explained that idea. It made a confusing topic feel simple." Notice how that lands. People light up. They remember it. And because it's rooted in truth, it never feels manipulative or cheesy.

Over time, these tiny, honest acknowledgments build stronger relationships at work, at home, and with friends. Compliments aren't fluff. They're one of the fastest ways to make interactions warmer.

Chapter 7: Be Flawed on Purpose

Back in 1966, psychologists Aronson, Willerman, and Floyd uncovered something that should make all the perfectionists among us breathe a sigh of relief. They found that highly competent people who slip up a little, who spill the coffee or trip over a word, become more likable, not less. It's called the Pratfall Effect, and it basically says people don't want to be around flawless statues. They want to be around humans. The polished, airbrushed version of ourselves might look impressive, but it doesn't connect. It might even be off-putting or intimidating. A tiny mistake, on the other hand, makes you feel relatable. Approachable. Someone others can actually exhale around.

This research exposes a quiet truth we all feel but rarely admit. Perfection is alienating. Vulnerability is magnetic.

When you let people see a small imperfection, you signal that it's safe to be real with you. Once people sense that, conversations get more honest, relationships soften, and you stop wasting energy trying to look flawless.

Tip 14: Let People See One Rough Edge

Perfection creates distance. Not always, but often enough. If every sentence sounds polished and controlled, people assume they have to be polished and controlled too. That's exhausting.

You don't need to overshare. Just stop sanding down every human edge. Say the small true thing: "I blanked on that this morning." "I had to redo it." "I totally missed that the first time." Then keep going. No apology spiral. No self-attack speech. Done right, this doesn't make you look less competent. It makes you feel safer to be around. People breathe a little when they realize they don't have to audition in front of you. One rough edge a day is enough.

Keep the delivery calm and the timing clean. Clarity beats extra wording.

Tip 15: Handle the Slip With Ease

A lot of us respond to mistakes by over-apologizing, spiraling, or launching into a long defense. That defeats the point. The power of the Pratfall Effect is not the mistake itself. It's how calmly you handle it.

When you stumble on a word, spill something, or get a fact slightly wrong, resist the urge to overcorrect. Add a quick smile or a simple "Welp, that's me today," then continue.

Treat the moment as an invitation for others to relax into their own humanity. You model comfort with imperfection, and that comfort spreads. People tend to trust that faster than polished perfection.

Research on authentic leadership and vulnerability points the same way: people trust you sooner when you stop pretending. One small honest line often lowers defensiveness and opens the room.

That's why being the first to share a small truth isn't oversharing. It's leadership.

Tip 16: Stop Managing Your Image

You don't have to dismantle your whole persona. Just loosen your grip a little. Image management is exhausting. You're constantly scanning for approval, rehearsing responses, and doing the whole "I've got it all together" act.

Vulnerability cuts through that noise. When you stop trying to look perfect, even briefly, people feel closer to you. And you feel closer to yourself.

Once a day, notice when you're tempted to sound smarter, cooler, or more put together than you feel. Then don't. Say the true thing instead. Admit you don't know. Admit you forgot. Admit you're learning. This open posture signals confidence, not weakness.

Over time, authenticity feels less like a tactic and more like relief. You show up without the costume.

It's like the conversation shifts from two people wearing armor to two people finally taking a breath. Once you try this a few times, you'll see why authenticity is such a strong social accelerator. People trust those who trust themselves enough to be real.

Chapter 8: Keep It Conversational

Back in 1974, conversation-analysis researcher Harvey Sacks dug into the mechanics of everyday talk and discovered something we all instinctively feel but rarely articulate. Natural conversation isn't a speech. It's a rally. It works best when people take quick, balanced turns, like a friendly game of table tennis. A short hit, a return, a rhythm you can feel in your bones. When one person starts hogging the ball, the whole thing collapses into a monologue, and everyone else mentally exits the chat.

Sacks and his colleagues found that the real glue of engaging dialogue is the back-and-forth. Short contributions, fast exchanges, little verbal volleys. You don't need to be brilliant. You just need to keep the ball in motion.

And the easiest way to do that is to keep your answers short, then pass the serve with a question or comment that opens the door for the other person. If you ever feel stuck, just lob the universal rally-saver: "So what do you think?" It works like magic because it hands the mic back and tells the other person you're actually interested.

Tip 17: Keep Responses Bite-Sized

If a conversation feels sluggish, chances are someone's talking in paragraphs. Don't be that person. Aim for responses that are short enough to keep momentum but long enough to add value. This isn't about delivering a TED Talk. You're just tossing the ball back. When you keep things brief, the other person feels invited instead of cornered. Practice answering questions in two or three sentences, then pivoting back with something that reopens the loop. "That's been my experience. How about you?" or "Yeah, it surprised me too. What was it like for you?" These tiny pivots build rhythm. They keep energy up. They turn a stiff exchange into something lively and collaborative.

Keep doing this and you'll notice people talk more freely around you because you create space instead of taking it.

Tip 18: Use Strategic Returns to Show Real Interest

If someone says, "The meeting was rough," and you respond with "Wow, yeah," the conversation stays flat. If you return one specific thread - "Rough how?" - now you're somewhere.

That's the whole move: return the detail, not a generic reaction. Catch one loaded phrase, hand it back as a short question, and stay there one beat longer than usual. "You said you almost quit. What was the moment?" "You called it chaotic. What part was worst?" It's not about running a technique. You're proving you heard them precisely. Most people never get that in everyday conversation, which is why this works so well.

Start with a familiar person, then test it in a slightly higher-stakes moment. That sequence builds fluency without making you sound scripted.

Once this habit is solid, your next move is how you open the interaction in the first two seconds.

Tip 19: Lead with a Soft Start

Think of your smile as the opening note of a song, not the entire performance. Those first two seconds are just about signaling "I'm safe, I'm here, I'm not about to emotionally tackle you." It's not about trying to dazzle anyone. You're simply choosing to land in the interaction on the warm side of neutral. A soft smile relaxes your jaw, softens your eyes, and tells the other person you're not in fight-or-flight mode. That alone is disarming in a world where most of us walk around looking slightly stressed and mildly late.

Next time you greet someone, give yourself one simple instruction: "Soft smile first, words second." Let the smile appear, hold it for a beat, then say what you were going to say anyway. No performance, no extra sparkle. Just reorder the sequence. You'll notice people respond with a little more ease.

Chapter 9: Use Their Name Wisely

There's one word that slices through background noise better than any other: your own name. You can be half checked out, scrolling your phone, pretending to listen to three things at once, and the second someone says your name, your attention snaps back like it was yanked on a string. Neuroscience research broadly supports this pattern. When people hear their own name, the brain's attention and emotional systems light up in a way that random words just do not.

It's like an internal notification that says, "Hey, this part is about you." Used well, a name is not a sales trick. It's recognition. It tells the other person, "I know who I'm talking to. You're not generic background noise."

The problem is we've all met the cartoon version of this technique: the person who uses your name every third sentence until it feels like you're in a customer service script. That's not the point. The real magic lives in a couple of natural, well-timed name drops that make the interaction feel personal instead of mechanical.

Tip 20: Use Their Name Twice

Think of a name as a spice, not the whole meal. You only need a small amount for it to change the flavor. Using someone's name early in the interaction helps lock in connection. Using it again later quietly reinforces that bond. That's all you need. Anything more starts to feel like a tactic you learned from a networking book you're a little too proud of. In your next conversation, say their name once in the first minute. "Nice to meet you, Rina," or "Good to see you, Marco." Then forget about it for a while.

Somewhere near the middle or end, drop it in again: "I liked what you said earlier, Rina," or "Thanks for sharing that, Marco." Two clean, honest uses. No more. You will notice the interaction feels warmer without ever dipping into cheesy territory.

Tip 21: Link Their Name to Something Real

A name alone is polite. A name plus a specific observation feels personal.

"Thanks, Maya" is fine. "Maya, the way you explained that made everything click" hits harder. Why? Because it sounds earned. It tells them you weren't on autopilot nodding through the exchange. Quick formula: name plus concrete behavior plus impact. "Jordan, you stayed steady there, and it kept the room calm." "Priya, your question made the decision clearer." Keep it short. Keep it true. Don't over-polish it. One clean line like this does more than five generic compliments. This tiny shift also helps people trust your praise. It no longer sounds like social filler. It sounds like attention.

Test this in one ordinary conversation today. If their shoulders drop or they open up, keep it.

Chapter 10: End Like an Invitation

Conversation is not just words. It's music. The rhythm, the volume, the way your sentences land all tell their own story. Linguistic research, including work by Elizabeth Couper-Kuhlen, suggests that a slight upward tone at the end of a sentence often signals openness. It's like you're putting a gentle question mark on the moment, even if your words are not technically a question. That small rise invites the other person to keep going, to add more, to step back into the space you just created. Used well, this rising tone turns your presence into something collaborative instead of closed. This isn't about delivering final verdicts. You're leaving doors cracked open. But there's a catch.

Push it too far and you slide into classic upspeak territory, where everything sounds uncertain and you start to sound like you're asking for permission to exist. The art here is control. Use the rising tone as a tool, not a default. When you choose your moments, you sound curious and inviting instead of unsure.

Tip 22: Let Some Sentences End Like Invitations

Not every line needs to sound like a question, but a few well-placed invitation endings can make a conversation feel easier to join. Think of it as leaving the door unlatched instead of bolting it with a period.

Use it on reflective lines, not on hard facts. "That got weird, huh?" works. "The meeting is at 3?" does not, unless you enjoy chaos. A slight upward finish can signal, "I'm open to your read," without making you sound hesitant. You still sound clear, just less closed.

Test it in one conversation where things feel flat. Say one observation with a gentle lift and then pause long enough for them to step in. The pause matters as much as the tone. If you rush to fill the space, the invitation gets canceled. Done right, this move makes your style feel more collaborative and less broadcast-heavy.

Tip 23: Match Curiosity with Confidence

The danger zone is when every sentence rises, no matter what you're saying. That's when you start to sound like you're apologizing for having a point of view. Rising tone works best as contrast. Use it to show curiosity, then let your voice land solidly when you're stating something you know or a boundary you mean.

Pay attention to your tone in one conversation. Use the upward lift only when you're inviting the other person in. When you're giving information, making a decision, or closing a thought, let your voice fall gently at the end. You're training yourself to sound confident and open at the same time. Not like you're handing your self-worth over for approval with every sentence.

Section: Attention & Listening

Up to this point, the focus was showing up with better social basics. From here on, the focus shifts to attention quality: what you notice, what you follow, and what you choose not to steamroll.

Listening isn't passive. It's directional. Where you place attention determines whether a conversation expands, stalls, or quietly collapses.

In this section, you'll focus on selective attention, pacing, and response restraint. The aim isn't to sound clever. It's to make people feel accurately heard, which is usually the hinge between polite conversation and real connection.

If conversations feel civil but thin, start here. These chapters help you catch what matters and respond in ways that keep trust moving forward.

Chapter 11: Ask One Better Follow-Up

Many people assume being good at conversation means having great stories ready to go. Nice, but not the main thing.

The stronger move is curiosity. In 2017, Harvard Business School researchers found that people who ask follow-up questions are rated as more likable, attentive, and enjoyable to talk to. Not because they're flashy, but because they make the other person feel interesting.

A follow-up question is a tiny act of generosity. You're saying, "I stayed with you past the headline."

Tip 24: Let Your Next Question Follow Their Last Line

The easiest way to ask better follow-ups is simple: pull your question from their last sentence, not from your own mental script.

Listen for one loaded word or phrase, then build from that. If they say, "It got messy," ask, "Messy how?" If they say, "I almost quit," ask, "What was the moment?"

This keeps the conversation flowing and makes people feel really heard. You're not jumping tracks. You're taking one step deeper on their track.

As this becomes a habit, people open up faster because they can feel you're tracking what actually matters to them.

That's where conversations shift from small talk to real talk. You don't need deep insights or therapy skills. You just need to keep caring for one sentence longer than usual.

Tip 25: Zoom In on One Detail

When people tell long stories, we usually do one of two things: interrupt, or drift. Better option: pick one meaningful detail and stay with it.

Not the whole story. One thread. Maybe it's the line they repeat. Maybe it's where their voice changes. Maybe it's one little moment they almost skip. That's your entry point. Ask a narrow question: "What changed right there?" "Why did that part stick with you?" "What made that decision hard?" Broad questions keep things vague. Narrow questions create depth without making it heavy. It's not about forcing intimacy. You're giving the conversation somewhere real to go. Most people answer these faster because the question feels manageable, not invasive.

Think of this as social muscle memory. A few consistent reps beat one perfect performance.

Tip 26: Let Their Answer Shape Your Next Move

A follow-up question is only half the move. The other half is what you do after they answer. Most people ask one decent question, then immediately yank the focus back to themselves. You can feel the gear shift. It turns the moment into a relay race where the baton keeps getting snatched away. Real connection happens when you let their answer steer what comes next. After you ask a follow-up, pretend your only job is to stay in their world for one more turn. Reflect something back. Ask a smaller follow-up. Or just say, "That makes a lot of sense," and pause. You're training yourself to resist the urge to recenter the conversation around you.

Soon, people start telling you more, trusting you more, and seeking you out more because you learned to ask one more sincere question.

Chapter 12: Tell It as a Scene

Facts are polite. Stories are sticky. You can list out all the bullet points, data, and logical reasons in the world, and people will nod along, then forget most of it by lunch. But tell one short, specific story, and it clings. Narrative research suggests stories are often far more memorable than data alone. The brain tags them as important because they come with context, emotion, and imagery.

In other words, stories feel like life. Facts often feel like homework. The good news is you don't need to become a master storyteller with dramatic arcs and plot twists. You just need story snapshots. Tiny scenes. One real moment that makes your point visible instead of theoretical.

A quick example from your life, your day, or something you observed in the wild. When you anchor your ideas in a story, people don't just understand you better. They carry what you said around with them longer, like a mental screenshot they can replay later.

Tip 27: Turn Your Point Into a Scene

Any time you're tempted to explain something abstract, ask yourself, "What is one moment that shows this in real life?" That's your story snapshot. It might be the first time you tried something and failed, a small win that surprised you, or a random Tuesday where this principle quietly showed up. One concrete moment beats ten clever explanations. The next time you're about to make a point, add a quick scene first. Instead of saying, "Following up with people matters," say, "Last week I sent one short message checking in with a client who had gone quiet, and they immediately re-engaged." Then you can add your takeaway. This isn't about adding fluff.

You're giving your idea a body so it can walk around in the other person's memory.

Tip 28: Keep It Short, Then Let It Breathe

The danger with stories is that they can sprawl. You start with a point, then suddenly you're five subplots deep and even you're tired of hearing yourself. A story snapshot should fit into a few sentences. Just enough detail to make it real, not enough to drag the conversation into a full documentary. Practice telling one story in under thirty seconds. Pick the moment, give only the essential details, and end with a clean line like, "That's when I realized…" Then stop talking. Let the other person react. They might ask a follow-up question, share their own story, or just sit with it. All of those are wins.

You offered something vivid and contained, which makes the interaction feel richer without hijacking the whole conversation. Closeness doesn't happen because two people dump their life stories on each other in record time. It happens in layers. In 1997, psychologist Arthur Aron and his colleagues found that gradually sharing personal thoughts and experiences can build surprisingly strong feelings of connection, even between strangers. That famous "36 Questions" study worked not because the questions were magical, but because they nudged people into taking turns revealing small, honest pieces of themselves. The small reveal is your everyday version of that. It isn't a dramatic confession or a trauma slideshow.

It's one genuine detail that gives the other person a peek behind your front-facing version. You're essentially saying, "Here is a tiny piece of the real me. What you do with it is up to you." Most people respond better than you expect. When handled gently, these little reveals create a feeling of "we" instead of two polished resumes talking at each other.

Tip 29: Share One True Detail

You don't build trust by dumping your whole backstory on someone in minute three. You build it by sharing one real detail that sounds like a human talking, not a bio.

A good test is this: could you say it in one breath? "I almost bailed before walking in." "I kept rewriting that message for twenty minutes." "I was trying to look calm, but I was spinning." That's enough. It's specific, it's honest, and it gives the other person something real to meet. Then stop. Let the moment breathe. When you overshare too fast, people feel pressure. When you share one true detail and leave room, people usually step toward you instead of away from you.

First attempts can feel clunky. Stay relaxed, keep it simple, and let repetition do the heavy lifting. Many people listen the way they watch trailers. They get the gist in the first few seconds, decide what they think, then spend the rest of the time waiting for it to end so they can react. The mirror and pivot technique interrupts that autopilot.

Communication models like motivational interviewing, developed by William Miller and Stephen Rollnick, are built on a simple idea: reflect a piece of what the person just said, then gently move the conversation forward. It's part echo, part curiosity. When you mirror someone's words, you're telling them, "I heard that part. That mattered." Their nervous system relaxes a little because they don't feel like they're talking into a void. Then the pivot invites them deeper. It's not about shoving the conversation in a new direction. You're following their thread a step further. Done well, it feels natural, almost invisible.

The magic lives in choosing one key word or short phrase and feeding it back to them. People usually pack their emotion into a small part of what they say. When someone tells you about something that happened, listen for the word that has the most weight. "I was exhausted by the end," or "It was awkward," or "Honestly, it felt huge." Pick that word and repeat it gently. "Exhausted?" or "Awkward how?" or "Huge in what way?" One echoed fragment, one small question. You'll be surprised how often they open up a layer deeper because you showed you were actually listening to the heart of it, not just the outline.

Tip 30: Pivot With Curiosity, Not Correction

Once you've mirrored their word or phrase, your next move decides the whole vibe. If you jump straight into advice, critique, or a comparison story about your own life, the moment closes. If you stay in curiosity mode, the conversation expands. The pivot should feel like you're turning the light slightly, not taking the spotlight for yourself. After you mirror, follow with a question that keeps the focus on their experience. "What do you think made it feel that way?" "What happened next for you?" "How are you feeling about it now?" Keep it simple and open. This isn't about interrogating them. You're walking beside them while they make sense of their own story.

Over time, people start to associate you with that rare feeling of being both heard and gently invited forward, and that's a great reputation to have.

Chapter 13: Leave on a High Note

Not every conversation is going to be perfect. Some will be awkward, rushed, or just okay. The good news is your brain doesn't keep a perfectly accurate record of the entire thing. Psychologist Daniel Kahneman's work on the "peak-end rule" suggests that people judge experiences mostly by two moments: the emotional high point and the ending. The rest sort of blurs. That means the last thirty seconds of a conversation carry way more weight than we think.

This chapter is about ending with meaning, not just politeness. You can't control every word that came before, but you can shape what the moment means as it closes.

You don't need a speech. You just need to land the plane gently instead of letting it nosedive into "Uh, anyway, I should go."

Tip 31: Name What Mattered

Right before a conversation ends, people tend to default to logistics. "I have to run." "Okay, cool." "See you." Functional, but flat. A stronger close is one quick line that names what actually mattered.

As you feel a conversation wrapping up, insert one simple line. "That part about your move really stuck with me." "Your take on that was sharper than I expected." "I'm leaving this clearer than I walked in." Then do your normal goodbye. You're not performing warmth. You're marking meaning. That's often the part their brain saves.

Land it with a steady tone and simple timing. Fewer words usually work better.

Tip 32: End with a Forward Pull

A lot of conversations end with a soft fade into nothing: "Alright, talk soon." Nice tone, no thread.

When you want the connection to continue, end with a gentle forward pull. One line is enough: "Send me that article when you find it." "I want to hear how that meeting goes." "Let's pick this up next week." This isn't about forcing a plan. You're giving the moment a small future. That's the difference between a pleasant chat and an actual relationship signal. Keep it light, realistic, and specific. If it sounds like an obligation, you've gone too far. If it sounds like genuine interest, you're right where you want to be.

Practice this first where the relationship is safe, then graduate to a tougher conversation. The step-up makes the habit feel natural, not performative.

Chapter 14: Listen with Your Face

People often think being a good listener is about what they do with their ears. It's not. It's about what they do with their face. While someone is talking, they're constantly scanning you for clues. Are you bored? Judgy? Confused? Secretly planning your grocery list?

Research on active listening by folks like Bodie and Fitch-Hauser found that small signals like nodding, soft eye contact, and responsive expressions make speakers feel more supported and connected. In plain terms, your face is either saying, "I'm with you," or "You're on your own." The wild part is you can be listening carefully on the inside and still broadcasting static on the outside. A blank, motionless expression can feel like a wall. An overly intense stare can feel like a spotlight. The listening face lives in the middle. Soft, engaged, tuned in. It's not about performing interest. You're just letting your actual attention show up on your face instead of hiding behind neutral.

Tip 33: Let Your Face Match Their Story

Your goal isn't to hold the same expression the whole time like a Zoom profile photo. Your goal is to let your face respond a little. If they tell you something painful, your face should soften. If they share a win, your eyes should brighten. This isn't about exaggerating. You're just allowing small, honest reactions to show up. That gives them emotional feedback that matches what they're sharing.

When you're listening, do a quick self-check. Ask yourself, "If someone froze my face right now, would it look like I'm listening?" If the answer is no, loosen something. Unclench your jaw. Soften your eyes. Let your eyebrows move a little. You don't have to act. Just stop hiding your reactions.

The tiniest shifts often make people feel a lot more understood.

Tip 34: Use Your Expression as Feedback

Your listening face isn't a prop. It's information. It tells the other person what it feels like to be heard by you. A couple of nods, a slight head tilt, a small smile at the right moment all say, "Keep going, I'm still here." Eyebrows can be surprisingly expressive and validating. That feedback matters more than any perfectly crafted response you're busy writing in your head while they talk. Pick one person today and decide you're going to give them better facial feedback for three minutes. Nod occasionally, mirror a bit of their emotion, let your face show when something is surprising or meaningful. Don't overdo it.

Think "present human," not "overexcited children's TV host." You'll notice the conversation feels smoother, and people often walk away feeling truly listened to.

Still, facial cues can be misread. If you're unsure whether you read them right, add a one-line clarity check: "So this feels frustrating?" or "Sounds like that mattered a lot to you." This turns silent guessing into shared understanding.

Psychologist Carl Rogers was big on this for a reason: when people hear their point played back accurately, defenses drop and trust goes up. Keep it short. Catch the center of gravity, then let them confirm or correct.

Tip 35: Treat Corrections as Progress

When someone corrects you after playing back the point, it's easy to hear "you failed." That's usually not what's happening. Most corrections are just course updates.

Handle them like steering, not judgment. "Good catch. Let me fix that." Then fix it and keep moving. No defensive speech. No self-flagellation. No five-minute explanation about how tired you've been. People trust the person who can adjust without drama. It makes you easier to work with and easier to talk to, because the room doesn't have to stop every time something is off by ten degrees. For one practice rep, use this in a low-stakes moment today and watch how quickly tension disappears when you treat correction like progress.

Try one small live rep today and track the reaction. A little relaxation on their side is your proof.

Chapter 15: Ask the Deeper Question

Most conversations never make it out of the shallow end. We trade headlines. "Work's busy." "The trip was good." "Yeah, things are fine." Technically, you talked. Emotionally, nothing really happened. Harvard researcher Alison Wood Brooks found that people open up more when they're asked questions that invite depth instead of just collecting more surface details. One well-aimed prompt can turn a flat recap into something real, without turning the moment into therapy in aisle three.

A deep-dive prompt isn't complicated. It's just a question that looks past the plot and goes for the meaning. Instead of "Then what happened?" you ask, "What made that stand out for you?" or "What was the most important part of that for you?"

You're gently steering the conversation from events to impact. That's where people reveal what they care about, what they fear, what they hope for. You know, the actual human stuff hiding underneath "Yeah, it was fine."

Tip 36: Ask What It Meant

We're trained to chase facts by default. Where did you go, who was there, how long did it last. That can keep a conversation alive, but it rarely makes it meaningful. The deep-dive prompt flips that. Even a simple question like "What did you like most about that?" forces the brain to sort, rank, and reflect. Ask for assessments, feelings, motivations, and so on.

Suddenly they're not just replaying the tape. They're making sense of it. When someone gives you the classic "Yeah, it was fine," don't chase the play-by-play. Go for meaning. "What part of that stuck with you the most?" Then stay quiet. Let them think. It might feel like a slightly heavier question at first, but people usually enjoy being asked it. You're giving them a chance to stop rushing and actually hear their own answer. That single prompt can make a three-minute chat feel oddly substantial.

Tip 37: Ask One Good Question, Then Pause

The temptation, once you see how well this works, is to start stacking deep questions like a podcast host. Please don't. Rapid-fire intensity makes people feel like they're under a microscope. The power of a deep-dive prompt comes from using it sparingly and then actually giving it space to land. One question, one pause, one genuine listen. Pick one conversation today and give yourself a strict rule. You get exactly one deep question. Make it a good one, something like "Why do you think that mattered so much to you?" After you ask, don't jump in to rephrase, soften, or fill the silence. Wait. Let them search for words. Let the answer arrive in its own time.

Very often, what they say next will be the most honest, interesting part of the entire interaction. And you'll be the person who made room for it.

Chapter 16: Name the Feeling Gently

A lot of us were never taught what to do with someone else's feelings. So we wing it. We change the subject, offer quick fixes, or crack a joke and hope it lands. The problem is, big emotions don't want to be fixed first. They want to be seen. UCLA researcher Matthew Lieberman's work suggests that simply putting feelings into words can actually calm the emotional centers of the brain. Naming what someone feels doesn't make it bigger. It often takes the sharp edge off.

That's where emotional labeling comes in. When someone shares a struggle, instead of launching into advice or reassurance, you reflect the feeling you hear. "That sounds frustrating." "That seems really disappointing." "You sound proud of that."

It looks small on the outside, but inside the other person's experience, it's huge. It says, "I'm not afraid of your feelings. I see them, and I'm staying." That kind of response is rare, and people remember who gives it to them. Unlabeled feelings behave like toddlers on espresso: louder, not clearer.

Tip 38: Name the Feeling, But Keep It Soft

Emotional labeling isn't about playing psychic. You don't have to nail the exact perfect word. You're just taking your best, gentle guess. The trick is to leave room for correction so it feels like an invitation, not a diagnosis. Phrases like "Sounds like...," "It seems like...," or "I get the sense that..." soften the edges and make it easy for them to say, "Yeah, exactly," or "Kind of, but it's more like this." The common mistake is going straight into fix-it mode. Better move? Respond with one short line that names what you think they might be feeling. "That sounds really draining." "It seems like that really hurt." Then stop. Let them confirm or adjust.

Either way, you just helped their brain organize what they're feeling, and you showed them you care enough to meet the emotion before you tackle the solution.

Tip 39: Let the Label Land

Naming a feeling works, but most people rush past the useful part. They label it and then sprint into advice.

Slow it down. Name it softly, then leave a little space. "That sounds frustrating." Pause. "That seems like a lot." Pause. The pause is not dead air. It's where the person feels the label land and decides whether they feel understood. If you jump in too fast, it feels like you're managing them. If you give it one beat, it feels like you're with them. Help can come after that. Usually better help, too, because you're solving the right thing instead of the first thing.

This pays off through consistency, not intensity. Small repeats quietly change how people feel with you.

Chapter 17: Match Depth, Not Drama

Human connection runs on a quiet rule that rarely gets announced out loud: when someone opens up, you feel a pull to meet them there. Social psychologist Alvin Gouldner called this the norm of reciprocity, and it shows up everywhere, especially in what people choose to share. One person reveals a little, the other responds with a little of their own. Not to keep score, but to keep balance. It's how conversations move from polite to personal without either person having to force it. The reciprocity reveal is about using that instinct on purpose. When someone offers you a small personal detail, you treat it like a tiny invitation instead of background noise.

You match it with something equally small and honest from your own world. Not a grand confession, not a dramatic monologue. Just a short, real moment that quietly says, "I trust you enough to show you a bit more of me." That kind of exchange builds closeness without feeling heavy, and it turns casual talks into actual relationships over time.

Tip 40: Match the Depth, Not the Drama

The aim isn't to "top" what they shared. In fact, escalating the vulnerability too fast can feel weird or attention-grabbing. The art is in matching the level. If they admit they still feel awkward at networking events, you might say, "Same, I usually feel a bit stiff at those too." If they mention being nervous about a new project, you could say, "I always get a little jumpy starting something new." This isn't about mirroring their exact story. You're mirroring the vulnerability level.

When someone shares something slightly personal, pause for half a second and ask yourself, "What's one small, honest thing I could share that lives in the same neighborhood as what they just said?" Offer that in one clean line. Then leave space. No overselling, no big explanation. You're simply placing your own small truth next to theirs and letting the symmetry do its quiet work.

Tip 41: Keep the Exchange Human

Reciprocity is a rhythm, not a contract. You're not obligated to spill your guts every time someone opens up, and you're not owed their story just because you shared yours. The aim is to create a feeling of mutuality, not to track who revealed what. When you treat sharing as a human gesture instead of a trade, people pick up on that safety. They feel like you're in this with them, not trying to pry something out. Start noticing the rhythm of disclosure in real time. Notice when they reveal something real, and check whether you're meeting that with equal honesty or hiding behind safe, polished lines.

If you catch yourself staying completely guarded while they're being real, let one small, true detail slip through. Nothing dramatic, just something honest. With practice, those tiny, balanced reveals stack into a sense of "we" that no amount of clever small talk can replace.

Section: Invitation & Curiosity

Once you can actually listen, the next move is inviting depth without pressure. This section is about creating openings people can choose, not traps they have to escape.

Depth doesn't arrive because you ask bigger questions. It arrives because people feel invited, not cornered.

These chapters focus on tone, timing, and framing: how to ask in a way that lowers pressure while increasing honesty. It's not about extracting information. You're building conditions where someone can choose to go deeper.

This section helps when conversations stay surface-level or transactional. The right kind of curiosity turns guarded exchanges into meaningful ones.

Chapter 18: Anchor the Moment

Some stories wander around like they're looking for parking. The person starts in one place, drifts to three subplots, takes a side road into childhood, then suddenly you're both lost and no one remembers the original point. It's not that they're bad at talking. Their brain just has too many tabs open. Psychologist Norbert Schwarz's work suggests that concrete anchors make thinking and communicating easier. When there's one clear reference point, everything else organizes around it.

A conversational anchor does that for real-time talk. You pick one specific detail from what they said and gently hook the conversation to it. Instead of chasing every branch of the story, you choose a single branch and say, "Let's look here." It sounds like, "When did that start?" or "How did you decide that?" or "What made that part so important?" Suddenly the fog lifts. They stop rambling and start articulating. This isn't about steering their story for them. You're just giving it a place to stand.

Tip 42: Anchor on One Detail

When someone talks, there's always at least one concrete thing you can latch onto. A date, a decision, a moment, a feeling. That's your anchor. You don't need to summarize everything they said. You just zoom in on that one piece and ask a grounded follow-up. "When did you first notice that?" "What made you choose that option?" "Where were you when that happened?" Specific questions calm scattered thoughts.

When the story starts wandering, plant a flag. Grab one single detail that feels solid. Ignore the rest for a second. Build your next question around that detail only. You'll often see their eyes focus, their words slow down, and their story become clearer. You didn't make them smarter.

You just handed their brain something steady to lean on.

Tip 43: Use Anchors to Help, Not Control

Anchors are supposed to help people find the thread again, not trap them in something they said fifteen minutes ago.

Use anchors like a map pin, not a courtroom exhibit. "Earlier you said timing was the main issue, is that still true?" That's useful. "But you said this before, so now you can't change it" is control dressed as consistency. Conversations are live. People revise their thinking as they talk. Good anchoring supports that. It keeps continuity without punishing movement. If your anchor makes the other person feel boxed in, it's not an anchor, it's a trap. Back up and use it to orient, not to win.

Don't worry if the first run feels unnatural. One honest rep at a time is how this starts sounding like you.

Another place anchors help is mismatch moments. Someone says one thing, but another detail points somewhere else. That usually means you just found the real thread.

Tip 44: Watch For Mismatch Moments

Mismatch moments are when the story doesn't quite line up yet. Timeline feels fuzzy. Emotion is high but details are vague. Or someone says, "It was fine," right after describing a complete mess.

Don't call this out like a gotcha. Use a calm anchor question. "Wait, which part felt worst?" "Was that before or after the deadline moved?" "When you said 'fine,' did you mean fine-fine or 'I'm holding it together' fine?" You're not trying to trap them. You're helping both of you get clearer.

If they start to shut down, simplify. One grounded question is enough. Done well, this turns confusion into clarity without making anyone feel cross-examined.

Chapter 19: Praise What They Did

Praise gets thrown around a lot, but a surprising amount of it is basically emotional confetti. "Great job." "You're amazing." "Love that." Nice to hear, sure, but it slides off because it's vague. Organizational psychologist Adam Grant and others have pointed out that people respond much more strongly when appreciation is specific. When you highlight one clear behavior instead of a broad trait, you're not just being nice. You're feeding their sense of competence and meaning. Their brain gets to say, "I did that. That mattered." Specific appreciation also signals something deeper: you were actually paying attention. You didn't just feel a vague positive vibe and throw a compliment at it.

You noticed the way they structured that email, or how they stayed calm in a tense moment, or how clearly they explained something confusing. That kind of recognition is about their thinking and choices, not just their existence. It respects the part of them that puts in effort. And when people feel seen at that level, they're far more likely to repeat the behavior and feel closer to you in the process.

Tip 45: Praise One Clear Behavior

Instead of telling someone they're great in general, zoom in on one thing they actually did. "You're so smart" is fuzzy. "I liked how you organized that so clearly" is sharp. "You're such a good friend" is nice. "I really appreciated how you checked in on me yesterday without making it a big deal" hits much harder. The more concrete you are, the more real it feels.

Pick one person today and swap out your usual generic praise for something specific. Watch what they did, then name that one action in a single sentence. "I noticed how you made that complicated thing easy to follow," or "Thanks for staying calm when everyone else was stressed, that really helped." Stop there.

No rambling, no overexplaining. You're letting the clarity of the observation do the heavy lifting.

Tip 46: Keep It Small and Real

A compliment gets stronger when it's smaller and more specific.

"Great job" is nice, but it fades instantly. "You explained that clearly and made the decision easier" lands and sticks. People can trust it because it points to something real they actually did. That's the whole goal: earned praise, not verbal confetti. Keep it to one behavior and one effect. No inflation. No speech. One line. It feels clean, and clean usually feels sincere. As a quick drill, give one specific compliment today that names what they did and why it mattered.

A calm voice and clean pacing do most of the work here. Don't over-explain.

Run your first reps with someone easy to talk to, then bring it into a more complex interaction. Confidence grows faster when the progression is deliberate.

Chapter 20: Bookmark and Return

People don't feel close to you just because you talk a lot. They feel close because you remember things. Tiny things. The project they were stressed about three weeks ago. The name of their dog. The random hobby they mentioned once in passing. When you bring one of those details back later, it hits like a quiet little compliment: "You mattered enough to stay in my head." That's a conversational bookmark. You mentally mark something they said, then flip back to it in a future chapter of the relationship. This isn't about having a photographic memory or treating people like a CRM system. It's about effort.

Plenty of folks can nod along for an hour and forget everything the second they walk away. Very few circle back with, "Hey, how did that thing go?" That gap is where warmth lives. Remembering even one specific thread tells the other person they're not just background noise in your life. They're a character you're actually following.

Tip 47: Revisit One Detail

A remembered detail lands best when it sounds casual, not investigative. This isn't about saying, "As recorded in our previous interaction..." You're just showing you carried something with you.

Simple examples work: "How did that presentation end up going?" "Did your sister visit after all?" "How's your dog doing after the surgery?" One sentence can do a surprising amount of relational work because it proves the last conversation didn't evaporate.

Before reaching out to someone, take five seconds and grab one thread from last time. Just one. You don't need a memory palace. Then open with it naturally and move on like it's normal, because it should be. This habit makes people feel remembered without making the moment heavy, and that's one of the fastest ways to make connection feel real. It quietly turns small talk into continuity, which most people are starving for.

Tip 48: Use Bookmarks to Show You're Here

Remembering details isn't just about being thoughtful. It also tells people they have continuity in your mind. You didn't drop them the moment they left your line of sight. That's especially powerful when it comes to things that felt vulnerable for them. Calling back to a challenge they shared or a risk they took says, "I didn't forget that mattered to you." It's not about prying. You're honoring. When you're wrapping up a conversation and someone mentions something important coming up, mentally tag it. A test. A deadline. A hard conversation. Then, the next time you talk, bring it up once. "I was thinking about that interview you had.

How did it go?" If they want to talk about it, they will. If they give a short answer, you can let it drop. Either way, you just proved you see their life as more than whatever's happening in front of you right now. That feeling of being remembered is one of the quietest, strongest forms of connection you can offer.

Chapter 21: Give Space First

A simple move is to feel when a conversation is off before a single word lands. Someone's standing just a bit too close, or hovering directly in front of you like a human pop-up ad, and your body quietly goes on alert. Anthropologist Edward Hall spent years studying this stuff and found that personal space isn't random. Distance and body angle shape how safe, relaxed, or trapped we feel in an interaction. When spacing is right, conversations flow. When it's wrong, even friendly words can feel tense. The tricky part is that personal space is invisible and deeply cultural. What feels warm and normal to one person can feel intrusive to another.

The social spacing rule is about noticing that invisible line and respecting it. When you give someone enough physical room and avoid squaring up like it's a standoff, their nervous system settles. They're more likely to talk freely, listen better, and stay present instead of subtly planning their escape route. Comfort creates bandwidth. Spacing is how you buy it.

Tip 49: Give Room Before Words

Before worrying about what to say, check where you're standing. A little distance goes a long way. Being about an arm's length away is a solid default in many casual settings, and angling your body slightly instead of facing someone head-on often feels less intense. It turns the interaction from "interrogation" into "conversation." Put this into play in a doorway moment, the hallway chat, the kitchen corner, the post-meeting linger. If you notice you're squared up like you're about to deliver a verdict, rotate your shoulders a few degrees and give yourself a sliver more space. You'll often see their posture loosen immediately. Same words, different distance, totally different vibe.

Use it once in a casual moment today. If the other person becomes easier and more open, it landed.

Tip 50: Let Them Set the Distance

Not everyone wants the same conversational distance. Some people are ready to go deep fast. Some need a few minutes to get there.

Your job is to notice and match before you push. Short answers, less eye contact, fewer questions back? Give space. Longer answers, more curiosity, relaxed body language? You can lean in a little. If you can't read it, ask lightly: "Want to keep going on this or switch gears?" That one line gives them control without killing momentum. People open faster when they feel they can choose the distance. You don't need to force depth. You need to make depth feel optional and safe.

Use it as a steady default, not a special-occasion move. The gain comes from doing it often.

Chapter 22: Signal the Turn

Conversations get awkward most often at the moment nobody talks about. The handoff. Two people circle the same pause, both unsure who's supposed to go next, and suddenly someone blurts something out a half-second too early. Cue the overlap, the apology, the tiny tension spike. Conversation analysis researchers like Emanuel Schegloff and Gail Jefferson found that smooth dialogue depends less on wit and more on how we signal turns. Humans rely on subtle markers to pass the conversational baton without dropping it. A conversational turn signal is simply a way to announce your move before you make it. Instead of cutting in or waiting so long the moment dies, you flag your intention out loud.

A short phrase like "Let me reflect that back," or "Here's what I'm thinking," gently shifts the floor to you. It reassures the other person that you're not hijacking the moment. You're stepping in with care. That clarity lowers defensiveness and keeps the exchange collaborative instead of competitive.

Tip 51: Signal Before You Step In

When you feel the urge to speak, especially after someone's shared something meaningful, give them a verbal heads-up. A brief signal buys you space without stealing it. It tells them, "I'm about to add something, and I respect what you just said." That alone changes how your words are received. Use an entry line before you add content. "Let me make sure I'm following," or "Can I share a thought?" "One thing I'm wondering…" Say that, then speak. It's a tiny courtesy that prevents your comment from landing like a takeover. You'll notice fewer interruptions, fewer defensive reactions, and more nodding instead of bracing. The words didn't get gentler. The transition did.

Awkwardness on the first few tries is part of the process. Keep it grounded and keep going.

Tip 52: Use Turn Signals to Lower Tension

Turn signals aren't about claiming the floor. They're about smoothing the transition. If they sound stiff or overly formal, they backfire. The aim is warmth and transparency, not dominance. A good signal feels conversational, not procedural. The mistake is waiting until the room gets tense, then forcing your way in. Pay attention to moments where conversations feel jumpy or tense, especially in groups. That's usually a turn-taking issue, not a content issue. Practice using natural, human signals like "One thing I'm wondering…" or "I want to build on that for a second." Soon people experience you as easy to talk with, not because you talk less or more, but because you move between roles smoothly.

Turn signals work best when verbal and nonverbal cues match. You make space, then you step in. That keeps conversations feeling respectful instead of rushed.

Your face matters in that handoff. Alex Todorov's research on first impressions highlights how fast people read expressions. So if your words are polite but your face looks tense, the transition can still feel sharp.

The neutral face reset prevents those accidental mixed signals.

Tip 53: Relax, Don't React

A neutral face isn't blank. It's soft. Jaw unclenched. Brows relaxed. Eyes engaged but not intense. Think "resting calm," not "resting stone statue." During a handoff, that gives the other person a safe surface to talk against. They don't feel evaluated. They feel received.

Do a quick internal scan when someone's talking and you're not actively responding. Jaw tight? Brows pulling together? Release them. Let your face settle. You're not performing warmth. You're removing tension.

Strong reactions can accidentally shut people down, even when you don't mean to. A calm, neutral expression says, "You can keep going. I'm not judging this." If you're unsure how to react, don't scramble for a face. Reset to neutral. Soft face, steady eye contact, relaxed posture. Let the moment breathe.

People tend to trust listeners whose faces feel stable, not performative. After enough reps, others speak more freely around you because your presence feels steady instead of reactive. That quiet steadiness is more reassuring than any perfectly timed smile.

Chapter 23: Start from Shared Ground

Connection gets a lot easier when you're standing on the same piece of ground. Shared experiences, even tiny ones, give conversations an instant sense of "we." It doesn't have to be a big event or a meaningful milestone. A meeting that dragged on. A weird moment in the elevator. The rain that caught you both without an umbrella. When you name something you both just lived through, you create a natural bridge into connection without forcing intimacy. These small callouts work because they highlight similarity. "We saw the same thing." "We were there together." That subtle sense of alignment lowers social friction fast. Instead of starting from zero, you're picking up from a point you already share.

The conversation feels warmer, easier, and more grounded because it's anchored in something real, not just polite small talk floating in the air.

Tip 54: Start Where You Both Already Are

Two people walk out of the same chaotic meeting and stand in the hallway pretending to reset. That is not the moment for a clever opener. It is the moment for shared reality. "That was a lot." "I did not expect that turn." One grounded line like that tells the other person you are in the same room with them, not performing social small talk.

Start where both of you already are, then see if it opens. If it does, great - you have traction. If it does not, you still landed as present instead of polished. You are not forcing depth; you are reducing friction. Most conversations get easier when the first line is obvious, honest, and tied to what just happened instead of what sounds impressive.

Tip 55: Use the Bridge and Go Deeper

The shared experience is the entry point, not the destination. Once it's named, you can gently step forward. Ask how it felt for them, what stood out, or what they thought about it. Because you're starting from common ground, the move toward depth feels natural instead of abrupt. After you name the shared moment, take one step forward, not five. "How did that land for you?" or "What was your take on it?" Keep it simple. Shared experiences create momentum because they remove the question of relevance. You're already talking about something that belongs to both of you. From there, deeper conversation doesn't feel like a leap. It feels like the next step across the bridge.

This lands best when you stay composed and concise. Let the signal carry the point.

Chapter 24: Ask Small, Ask Clear

There's a quiet shift that happens when you ask someone for their opinion. The energy changes. They sit up a little. Their brain leans in. Self-determination researchers Edward Deci and Richard Ryan have found that feeling competent and having agency are core psychological needs. When you make a small ask, you're tapping straight into that. You're saying, "Your perspective matters here." That lands deeper than most compliments ever will.

The key is keeping it small and sincere. This isn't about outsourcing your decisions or fishing for validation. It's about inviting someone into the process in a low-pressure way. A simple request for input turns a one-sided interaction into a shared moment.

Respect starts flowing both directions, because people feel seen not just as listeners, but as contributors.

Tip 56: Ask for Input, Not Permission

A small ask works best when it's framed as curiosity, not uncertainty. There's a difference between "I have no idea what I'm doing, help" and "I'd love your take on this." The second one signals confidence and openness at the same time. It's not about handing over control. You're widening the lens.

Give yourself a low-pressure quota: one small ask per day. "What would you do here?" "Does that make sense to you?" "I'm curious how you see this." Keep it light and specific. Then shut up and let them take the mic. You'll notice people respond with more energy and care, because you just gave them a role instead of an audience seat.

People perk up when they feel useful.

Tip 57: Let Their Answer Matter

Nothing deflates a small ask faster than ignoring the answer. If you ask for someone's input, treat it like it counts, even if you don't end up using it. Acknowledge it. Consider it out loud. Thank them for it. That follow-through is what turns a polite question into real respect.

After someone shares their perspective, don't let their answer hit the floor. Catch one part of it out loud. "That's a good point," or "I hadn't thought about it that way." You're not required to agree or comply. You're showing that their contribution landed. Even if you choose a different route, acknowledging the input is what makes the ask feel respectful instead of performative.

Over time, people feel more invested around you, because you're not just asking for their thoughts. You're making space for them.

Chapter 25: Lean In with Curiosity

Interest is felt long before it's explained. When someone's sharing something that matters to them, their body is watching yours for cues, even if neither of you is consciously aware of it. Research on nonverbal immediacy suggests that small forward movements signal engagement and warmth. A slight lean says, "This matters. I'm here with you." It's subtle, but the nervous system picks it up instantly. Body language is rarely neutral. It's almost always communicating welcome or distance, attention or disengagement. The curiosity lean works because it closes psychological space without crowding physical space. This isn't about stepping into their bubble or hovering over them.

You're shifting your posture just enough to show that your attention has moved from passive to active. It tells the other person they're not talking into the air or competing with your thoughts. In moments where someone is deciding whether to keep sharing or pull back, that tiny lean can be the difference. It's often the signal that tips them toward opening up instead of shutting down.

Tip 58: Lean In When It Deepens

Before: someone says, "Can I be honest?" and you keep your body exactly the same - same posture, same speed, same half-listening face. They usually pull back.

After: they hit that deeper turn, and you make one small shift. Lean in a little. Soften your expression. Stop talking. That tiny adjustment reads as, "I am with you for this part." It is not dramatic, and that is why it works.

You are not leaning in all conversation long like a motivational speaker in a documentary. You are responding to the moment that actually needs it. If you time it right, people keep going. If you miss it, they usually edit themselves mid-sentence. Watch for those threshold phrases - "Honestly..." "This might sound weird..." - and let your posture do the invitation.

Tip 59: Let the Lean Replace the Interrupt

A lot of interruptions come from good intentions. You want to show understanding, agreement, or empathy, so you jump in with words. The curiosity lean lets you show all of that without breaking their flow. It's a way to encourage without redirecting, to affirm without taking over. Swap the verbal interruption for a physical one. Instead of "Yeah, totally" or "I get that," lean in instead and nod once or twice. Hold eye contact. Let them finish. You're giving them space while still showing engagement. With practice, people will start to experience you as someone who actually lets thoughts land, not someone who rushes past them.

Run this in a low-friction relationship first, then apply it where the stakes are a bit higher. You'll keep the quality while stretching your range.

Chapter 26: Align on the Goal

Disagreements don't usually blow up because people want opposite things. They blow up because each person feels like the other one is standing in their way. Once that frame sets in, every sentence starts sounding like a challenge. Harvard negotiator Roger Fisher's work suggests that one of the fastest ways to lower defensiveness is to step out of the "me versus you" setup entirely and name what both of you actually want. When the goal becomes shared, the tension drops almost immediately. The shared goal frame works by shifting attention to a third thing. Not you. Not them. The outcome.

When you say out loud what you are both trying to achieve in that moment, you stop wrestling over positions and start standing on the same side of the table. Even if you still disagree on how to get there, the emotional tone changes. You are no longer opponents. You are collaborators with different ideas. That difference matters more than most people realize.

Tip 60: Name the Goal Before You Argue the Details

When tension shows up, people often jump straight into defending their point. That usually locks the other person into defending theirs. A shared goal frame slows that spiral. Before pushing your perspective, you name the common aim. "I think we both want this project to go smoothly." "It sounds like we both want a solution that's fair." "We're both trying to make this easier, not harder." When friction rises, pause and say one sentence that names what you believe you both care about in that moment. Use one line that puts you on the same side of the table: "We both want this to go smoothly." "We're aiming for something fair here." Then move into your point.

Keep it straightforward and genuine. If they agree, great. If they tweak it, that's still progress. Either way, you've just moved the conversation out of combat mode and into problem-solving mode.

Tip 61: Use the Goal, Not a Weapon

The shared goal is not something you bring up once and then ignore. It becomes the reference point you both return to. When things drift back toward tension, you gently loop it in again. "Does this move us closer to what we said we wanted?" or "How does this option support that goal?" It's not about using the goal to corner them. It's to keep the conversation oriented forward. If you notice yourself getting pulled back into proving your side, redirect by pointing to the shared aim instead of the disagreement. This keeps the focus on solutions rather than blame. People are far more willing to compromise when they feel like they're protecting something together instead of giving something up.

Give this one clean attempt today in a low-pressure exchange. If tension drops, you're on track.

Chapter 27: Ask for Their Thinking

Tension often shows up not because someone's choice was wrong, but because their reasoning is invisible. When you don't understand why someone did what they did, your brain fills in the blanks, and it usually doesn't do them any favors. Psychologist John Gottman's research on conflict communication suggests that curiosity is one of the strongest antidotes to defensiveness. When people feel judged, they brace. When they feel understood, they explain. That difference changes everything. Intentional inquiry is the practice of asking about someone's thinking without putting them on trial. This isn't about cross-examining or subtly trying to expose a flaw. You're opening a door. A question like, "What led you to that choice?"

or "How were you thinking about that at the time?" invites context instead of confrontation. It slows the emotional temperature and shifts the conversation from accusation to understanding. Even when you still disagree, the tone becomes steadier and more human.

Tip 62: Ask for Thinking, Not Defense

"Why did you do that?" sounds neutral in your head. In their ears, it often sounds like court.

Give this swap a shot: "Walk me through what made that seem right at the time." "What were you weighing in that moment?" "What outcome were you hoping for?"

Same topic. Different energy. You are asking for thinking, not demanding a defense. That keeps people in explanation mode instead of self-protection mode, which means you actually learn something useful.

If you go in hot, you get polished answers. If you ask for process, you get reality. You can still disagree after that. In fact, disagreement goes better once both people are reacting to what actually happened instead of reacting to tone. You end up debating substance, not posture.

Tip 63: Let Curiosity De-Escalate

Intentional inquiry works best when it's paired with genuine restraint. If you ask a thoughtful question and then immediately counter their answer, the safety disappears. The aim is not to collect information so you can win. It's to understand enough that the conversation doesn't collapse into defensiveness. Curiosity lowers the stakes because it tells the other person they don't have to fight to be heard. After asking an inquiry question, give their answer your full attention for one full turn. Reflect one part of what you heard before offering your view. Even a simple "That helps me see where you were coming from" can soften the exchange.

Do this consistently and people start to experience you as someone who seeks understanding before judgment. That reputation makes difficult conversations easier before they even begin, because others trust that you're not there to corner them.

Chapter 28: Change the Story Mid-Thought

Emotions aren't the problem. Speed is. Most conversational blowups don't happen because something truly awful occurred, but because the brain grabbed the first interpretation it could find and ran with it. Stanford psychologist James Gross's work suggests that cognitive reappraisal, meaning changing how you interpret a moment, can significantly reduce emotional intensity. The catch is timing. You can't reframe while you're already reacting. You need a beat. The cognitive reframe pause is that beat. It's the small space between stimulus and response where you step off autopilot. Instead of firing back from assumption, you ask yourself a quieter, steadier question: "What else could this mean?" Maybe that comment wasn't a dig. Maybe that silence wasn't disapproval.

Maybe that tone had more to do with their stress than your worth. It's not about gaslighting yourself or ignoring red flags. You're widening the lens before you decide what story you're going to tell yourself. That pause often saves conversations that would've otherwise gone sideways.

Tip 64: Interrupt the First Brain Story

Your brain is excellent at speed and terrible at nuance when emotions are involved. It grabs the fastest explanation, and that explanation usually stars you as either the victim or the villain. The reframe pause slows that down just enough to introduce alternatives. This isn't about deciding which story is true yet. You're just refusing to marry the first one that shows up. The moment you feel a spike of irritation, embarrassment, or defensiveness, don't answer the person yet. Answer your brain. Come up with two alternative explanations (don't have to be better), even boring ones.

"I don't have enough context." "They're distracted." This simple move often lowers the emotional charge enough that your response comes out calmer, clearer, and far less regrettable.

Tip 65: Reframe to Neutral First

Reframing doesn't mean forcing optimism. Jumping straight to "They meant well" can feel fake and unsatisfying when you're upset. A more realistic move is aiming for neutral first. Neutral interpretations calm the nervous system without requiring you to pretend everything's fine. From there, genuinely positive interpretations become possible instead of forced. Start with neutral lines you can actually believe: "I might be missing something" or "This might not be about me." Let that settle before you speak. If a more generous interpretation naturally follows, great. If not, you still avoided reacting from assumption. With practice, this habit turns you into someone who responds instead of reacts, even under pressure. And that steadiness changes how people experience you.

Conversations feel safer, conflicts cool faster, and you keep your self-respect intact without swallowing your feelings or lighting the match too fast.

Section: Guiding the Interaction

Invitation gets people in. Guidance keeps the conversation useful once you're both inside it. This section is about steering lightly so momentum doesn't collapse.

Good conversations don't need control, but they do need direction. Without it, they drift, loop, or lose energy.

This section is about light steering: shaping pace, transitions, and clarity without taking over. The emphasis is collaboration, not dominance.

If a conversation keeps circling the same points, these chapters help you restore momentum while keeping the other person fully in the process.

Chapter 29: Close with Gratitude

How a conversation ends often matters more than what filled the middle. You can have a thoughtful exchange, useful feedback, or even a mild disagreement, and the final note is what sticks. Chapter 13 covered ending with meaning. This chapter is the explicit appreciation version of that close.

Psychologist Robert Emmons' research on gratitude suggests that expressing appreciation boosts positive emotion for both the person giving it and the person receiving it. A simple thank-you doesn't just feel polite. It leaves the nervous system in a better place. The gratitude close is about finishing strong without being sentimental or over the top. It's not about delivering a speech or wrapping things in a bow. You're just naming something you genuinely appreciated before you part ways. That small act reframes the entire interaction as worthwhile.

Even if the conversation was brief or slightly awkward, gratitude can soften the edges and give it a warmer aftertaste. People often remember how you made them feel more than what you said, and appreciation is one of the cleanest ways to leave a good feeling behind.

Tip 66: Thank Them for Something Specific

Most thank-yous are polite and forgettable. "Thanks" lands, then disappears. To make it stick, thank the exact thing they gave you.

"Thanks for staying patient while I sorted that out." "I appreciate how direct you were - that helped."

"Thanks for giving me the full context instead of the short version."

That kind of line feels different because it is specific and earned. You are not handing out generic warmth. You are showing you were paying attention. And that felt attention is exactly what people remember long after the details fade.

Quick rule for endings: before you leave, ask yourself, what did they give me in this conversation? Clarity? Time? Honesty? Name that. It takes three seconds and usually changes how the whole interaction gets remembered.

You get returns here through regular practice. Keep it light and repeatable.

Tip 67: Let Gratitude Be the Last Word

The power of the gratitude close comes from placement. If you thank someone and then immediately pile on a new request or criticism, the effect gets diluted. Gratitude works best when it actually closes the loop. You're saying, "This was enough. I value it." That finality is what makes it feel sincere instead of transactional. Experiment with ending one conversation today with appreciation and nothing else. No extra ask, no "also one more thing," no soft re-entry. Just appreciation, then exit. "Thanks for your time, that was really helpful." "I appreciate you taking a minute to talk." With practice, people will start associating you with interactions that feel complete and respectful, not draining or unfinished.

That reputation quietly opens doors, because everyone prefers conversations that end with warmth instead of friction or fade-out silence.

Chapter 30: Set the Tone Early

Some conversations feel tense before the first hard sentence lands. The room has already tilted defensive. That isn't random; it's usually the result of how the interaction was framed in the opening seconds. Psychologist John Bargh's work on priming suggests that what people are exposed to first can nudge what they notice, how they interpret things, and how they behave, often without realizing it. In normal-person terms: the opening of an interaction tilts the whole table. If you start with stress, urgency, or a complaint, you've basically poured hot sauce into the first 10 seconds. Even if the topic is fine, the mood is now on alert.

Start with warmth, curiosity, or simple cooperation, and the opposite happens. People loosen up. Replies get less defensive. Hard topics land with less friction because the emotional context gets set before the content arrives.

This isn't manipulation. It's choosing whether the conversation begins like a handshake or a surprise audit.

You've felt this in real life. Someone opens with "We need to talk," and your stomach does a small cartwheel. Same topic, different opener, and your whole body reacts differently.

The first line doesn't have to be poetic. It just has to be intentional.

Tip 68: Lead with the Tone You Want

For a calm conversation, start calmly. For collaboration, open collaboratively. The mistake many people make is sprinting straight into the point like the point is a grenade and everyone needs to look at it right now. Then they're surprised when the other person flinches. A better move is a two-step opening: tone first, topic second. Tone is the part where you signal goodwill. Topic is the part where you bring the actual thing. This can be ridiculously small. One sentence.

Here are a few openers that set a clean tone without sounding like a motivational poster: "I'm glad we're talking about this." "I want to make this easy to sort out." "I'm curious what your take is." "Quick check-in before we get into it."

Notice what those do. They don't soften the issue. They soften the landing. They tell the other person you're here to solve, not to win. Concrete thing to try: before you start a conversation, pick one word for the vibe you want (calm, clear, cooperative, honest). Then pick an opening line that matches it. You'll sound steadier, and you'll feel steadier, because you're not throwing your nervous system into a sprint right out of the gate.

Tip 69: Prime Before You Problem-Solve

A lot of conversations go sideways because the problem shows up before the relationship does. Someone opens with the issue cold, like, "Why didn't you do this?" or "We need to fix that," and suddenly the other person is defending themselves before they even understand what's being asked. The content might be reasonable, but the order is backwards.

Priming is simply establishing partnership before you introduce friction. It's the difference between: "Here's what's wrong." and "Let's get aligned, then handle what's wrong." That "let's" matters. It's a tiny linguistic shift that changes the shape of the room. This isn't about asking for permission. It's not about buttering anyone up.

You're making it clear you're on the same side of the table before you start moving pieces around. Use a cooperative frame that still sounds like you: "I want us on the same page." "Can we figure this out together?" "I'm trying to understand what happened so we can fix it." Then bring the issue in plain language. No dramatic wind-up. No sneaky accusation disguised as a question. A simple real-life script for something sensitive: "Quick check-in. I want us aligned." "Here's what I'm seeing." "Can you walk me through your side?" That's it. Three lines.

Chapter 31: Make Them Feel Heard

You've met this person. You bump into them for "two minutes" and somehow you end up telling them about your childhood haircut trauma, your secret hobby, and the fact that you're considering a career change because your inbox now has its own weather system. You walk away thinking, Wow, they're so interesting. Plot twist: they didn't do anything flashy. They just made it weirdly easy for you to talk.

Psychologist Diana Tamir's research on self-disclosure points to a simple reason this works. When people talk about themselves, especially about things that matter, reward-related systems in the brain can light up. Not because everyone is a narcissist. Because being understood is soothing.

So when someone gives you room to speak and actually stays with you, your brain links that relief to them. You don't walk away remembering their perfect story. You walk away remembering the ease.

You see this in tiny moments. Someone asks, "How've you been?" and you give the polite answer. Then they ask one real follow-up and suddenly you're honest. Or they cut in with their own story and your internal shutters close.

The speaker favor effect is simple: people like the person who makes being heard feel good.

Tip 70: Find the Spark and Fan It

Field note: when someone comes alive in conversation, most people accidentally smother it by changing topics too fast. They hear enthusiasm and immediately steer back to logistics, or to themselves.

Better move: fan the spark once. Ask one curiosity-forward question and stay there for thirty extra seconds. "What made you choose that?" "What part of it are you enjoying most?" "What surprised you once you started?"

You do not need a whole segment. Just one extra turn where you let their interest breathe. That is usually enough for the conversation to shift from polite to real. That extra half-minute is often where the useful truth finally appears.

If they do not want to go further, they will naturally taper. No harm done. If they do, you just found the thread worth following.

Tip 71: Let Them Finish the Thought

A common social reflex is "matching." Someone shares something meaningful and you rush to show you relate by telling your own version. It comes from good intentions, but it often lands like competition. Here's the test: are you adding to their experience, or replacing it with yours? If they say, "I finally finished that project," and you respond with, "Oh my god, same, I've been drowning in work," the spotlight just moved. They'll smile, but the moment is gone. The reward got interrupted. Try a "one more turn" rule instead. When someone is sharing something they care about, give them one extra lap before you bring in your story.

You could do it in three easy moves: Reflect: "That sounds like a huge relief." Follow up: "What was the turning point?" Let them finish: hold the silence for a beat so they can complete the thought. Only after that do you share your piece, and keep it short. Think garnish, not entree. The result is subtle but real. People feel fully heard, not half-heard. The conversation feels like it has room, not like it's constantly being redirected. And over time, people start seeking you out because being around you feels good in the simplest way: they get to be themselves without fighting for space. Group conversations have a predictable villain: momentum.

One person jumps in, someone laughs, another person adds a story, and suddenly the pace is so fast that quieter people never get a clean entry point. They're not uninterested. They're just out of oxygen. Conversation analyst Harvey Sacks's work suggests that turn-taking follows patterns even when talk feels casual. In groups, those patterns get noisy fast, and the quickest speakers often win by default. Thoughtful people, especially those who need an extra beat to form a sentence, can get sidelined without anyone meaning to do it. The floor gift is your small correction to that drift.

You create one deliberate opening: "Wait, I want your take," or "Hold on, what were you about to say?" Then you stop long enough for them to step in. It's a tiny move, but it balances the room immediately and marks you as someone who includes people, not just airtime.

Tip 72: Make It an Invitation

Giving someone the floor shouldn't feel like a spotlight they didn't ask for. Tone matters. Your invitation should feel optional and warm, not like a pop quiz. A relaxed delivery and open body language help people step in without anxiety. Watch how people respond after you offer the floor. If they hesitate, soften the moment. "No pressure, just if you want to share." You're communicating that their voice is welcome, not required. With practice, people will associate you with conversations that feel balanced and inclusive. You become the person who doesn't just talk well, but creates space well. And that's a skill people notice and trust quickly.

Early reps may feel mechanical. That passes quickly once you use it in real conversations.

Chapter 32: Share, Don't Spill

Vulnerability works, but only when it fits the moment. Dumping your entire inner world into a casual conversation doesn't build trust, it builds discomfort. What actually strengthens connection is relevance. A 2015 study by psychologists Collins and Miller found that modest, well-timed self-disclosures increase likability and closeness. The key word there is modest. People respond best when what you share feels connected to what's happening right now, not like a surprise emotional monologue. Selective vulnerability is about choosing which truth to share, not sharing everything. You offer a small, specific piece that matches the tone and depth of the interaction. That move quietly says, "I'm real with you, and I know where the edge is."

It invites mutual openness without forcing it. When done well, it creates familiarity fast because the other person senses you're present, human, and emotionally calibrated, not performing or oversharing.

Tip 73: Share What's Relevant

Trust doesn't grow from intensity alone. It grows from alignment. If the conversation is about uncertainty, share a moment where you felt unsure. If it's about learning, share something you're still figuring out. The power comes from relevance, not emotional weight. A line like, "I remember feeling pretty lost my first time doing that," often lands better than a dramatic confession that doesn't match the moment. Before sharing something personal, ask yourself, "Does this connect directly to what we're talking about?" If the answer is yes, keep it short and honest. One or two sentences is plenty. You're offering context, not asking for caretaking. That balance is what makes people feel safe instead of overwhelmed.

Use a quiet tone and deliberate timing. The move works because it's clear, not because it's long.

Tip 74: Stop Before You Explain

Right after a vulnerable line, people often panic and start cleaning it up. "Sorry, that sounded dramatic." "I do not usually say stuff like that." That self-editing kills the moment you just opened.

Try not doing that. Share the thing, then leave it alone. Let it stand for two beats. If the room is quiet, let it be quiet. You do not have to rescue your own honesty.

This is harder than it sounds, mostly because over-explaining feels safer in the short term. But when you stop cushioning every real sentence, your vulnerability reads as grounded instead of needy. People trust that faster.

One practical rep: the next time you share something personal, do not add a disclaimer after it. Just stop and see what happens.

Chapter 33: Check the Emotional Weather

Conversations don't usually fall apart with a bang. They drift. A little stiffness here, a little guardedness there, until something feels off and no one knows why. Yale researcher Marc Brackett's work on emotional intelligence suggests that naming emotional context improves communication and reduces misunderstanding. When feelings stay unspoken, people guess. And guessing is where tension quietly grows. The emotional temperature check is a gentle way to bring the unspoken into the room before it turns into friction. This isn't about stopping the conversation to analyze it. You're simply checking alignment. A soft question like, "How are you feeling about this so far?" or "Does this feel okay to talk about?" shows care and awareness.

It signals that you're paying attention not just to the topic, but to the human experience happening alongside it. That alone can ease defensiveness and invite honesty.

Tip 75: Check In Before Things Get Weird

The best time to check the temperature is when you feel the first signs of drift, not when someone's already shut down.

What it can look like: - Their energy drops or tightens. - They answer in shorter sentences. - They stop asking questions back. - Their body turns slightly away (the classic slow exit).

What to say: - "How's this landing for you?" - "Are we good to keep going?" - "Do you want to keep talking about this, or switch gears?"

How to say it: - Calm tone. - Neutral face. - No "you seem upset" accusation energy.

A check-in doesn't have to be deep. It just has to be early.

You're giving the other person a clean opening to tell the truth before the tension hardens into a story.

Tip 76: Treat the Answer as Data

Once you ask, the real skill is not panicking when you get a real answer. If they say they're confused, overwhelmed, or uncomfortable, that's not the conversation failing. That's the conversation finally getting honest. Listen to their answer without defending yourself or rushing to smooth it over. A simple response like, "Thanks for telling me," or "Okay, that helps" keeps the space safe. From there, you can ask what they need or suggest a small shift like slowing down, clarifying what you meant, taking a break, changing the setting, or just asking what they need. The aim is to keep the conversation from drifting into silent guessing, because silent guessing is where people start building resentment like it's a hobby.

Over time, people experience you as someone who notices emotional undercurrents and addresses them with care instead of avoidance. That makes conversations steadier, safer, and more human, because you're responding to what's actually happening, not what you hope is happening.

Chapter 34: Be the Calm in the Room

Have you ever noticed how one person's mood can hijack an entire room? Someone walks in tense, speaking fast, voice a little sharp, and suddenly everyone else starts talking a little faster too. Not because they decided to, but because the vibe is contagious. Humans are basically emotional Wi-Fi. We connect automatically. Research on emotional contagion and regulation backs this up, and work associated with researchers like Robert Levenson suggests something hopeful: one person's steadiness can lower the other person's reactivity during a difficult interaction. Calm can spread the same way tension does. Quietly. Through tone, pace, posture, and facial expression. Not through a lecture about staying calm, which usually makes the other person want to throw a chair.

That's the idea behind the regulation spillover cue. Instead of trying to manage the other person's feelings directly, you manage your own state in a way they can feel: slower pace, softer face, less reflexive fixing or defending.

This isn't passive or emotionless. It's choosing not to add gasoline to a moment that already has enough heat.

Most tense conversations don't need more logic right away. When someone is worked up, their brain is scanning for threat, not nuance. Match that intensity and you get a tug-of-war. Bring grounded steadiness and the tug often loosens.

Tip 77: Slow the Moment by Slowing Down

The instinct under tension is speed. Talk faster, explain harder, make your point airtight before you get interrupted. That urge is understandable, and it usually makes things worse. A steadier move is to reduce your speed on purpose. Not dramatically, not like you're acting in a mindfulness commercial. Just enough that your next sentence doesn't come out like a reflex. Take one full breath before you respond. Let your words arrive at a slightly slower pace. Lower your volume a notch. Keep your gestures smaller. You'll feel the difference in your body first. Your chest loosens. Your jaw unclenches. Your thoughts get less scattered.

And because people unconsciously mirror each other's pacing, the other person often starts matching you without realizing it. The conversation doesn't magically become pleasant, but it becomes more workable. You've turned down the heat enough for actual understanding to have a chance.

Tip 78: Make Calm Look Like Presence

Calm can look fake when it turns into a performance: frozen face, clipped voice, and that tight "I am totally fine" smile that convinces no one.

Presence looks different. You are still human in your face, just not reactive in your pace. Shoulders down. Breath slower than usual. Eyes on the person, not scanning for exits. You can nod, pause, and answer without turning the moment into theater.

If you need an anchor, make it physical: feel both feet on the floor and lengthen one exhale before you respond. It is boring, but it works. The target is steady and warm, not steady and emotionally unavailable.

After enough reps, people read you as steady under pressure. Not detached. Not performatively zen. Just steady enough that difficult conversations do not instantly become emotional pileups.

Chapter 35: Assume Good Intent First

Conflict often isn't caused by what someone did. It's caused by what we assume it meant. Social psychologist Shelley Taylor's research on attribution suggests that the explanations we choose shape emotional reactions and outcomes. When we assume negative intent, our tone tightens, our defenses rise, and the conversation hardens. When we assume good intent, even temporarily, the entire exchange softens. The positive assumption frame is a starting posture, not blind optimism. It's not about denying harm or pretending everything's fine. You're choosing not to assign malicious motives without evidence. That single decision changes how you sound, how you listen, and how the other person responds. People can feel when they're being approached with suspicion versus generosity. One invites explanation.

The other invites battle.

This chapter works best when you treat it like a live experiment, not a rulebook. Try one move in one real conversation, then notice what changes in tone, pace, and trust.

Tip 79: Pause Before You Assign Motive

The brain loves fast stories, especially under stress. Someone interrupts, forgets to reply, or says something awkward, and your mind jumps straight to "They don't respect me." Pause that jump. Before assigning motive, force three neutral explanations: they were distracted, they misunderstood, or it had nothing to do with you. You don't have to fully believe those options. You just have to let them exist long enough to lower the heat.

Begin where trust already exists, then use the same move in a harder setting. That transition is how skill becomes reliable under pressure.

Tip 80: Let the Assumption Shape Tone

Even when you never say your assumption out loud, it leaks through your tone. Suspicion sounds sharp. Generosity sounds open. If you assume the other person probably meant neutral or well-intended, your voice softens and your questions land as curiosity instead of accusation. That alone can prevent a defensive spiral before it starts.

Use this swap in real time: replace "Why did you do that?" with "Can you walk me through what was happening there?" Same topic, very different signal. People explain more honestly when they don't feel cross-examined. Do this a few times and you become the person who handles misunderstandings without turning them into fights.

Tip 81: Give Them a Role to Step Into

People usually move toward the role they feel is being seen. That positive expectation effect is old research and everyday reality. If someone feels treated like a capable contributor, they usually show up that way. If they feel treated like a problem, they get guarded fast. So make the role explicit in one grounded line.

Name a strength you've actually seen, then invite it in: "You're great at spotting practical issues. What do you see here?" or "You usually catch the detail I miss. What am I missing?" It's not flattery confetti. It's a door. You're setting a useful expectation and giving them room to meet it.

Tip 82: Keep It Clean, Then Hold Space

Micro-validation works because it's light. One clean line is enough: "That makes sense," "I get why that was frustrating," or "Yeah, that would throw me too." Then stop. If you stack five reassurance lines, it starts sounding fake. Say one real sentence, then hold a beat and let them continue.

Key distinction: validate the feeling, not the verdict. You can acknowledge "that sounds rough" without agreeing with every conclusion they drew. That keeps the moment safe without becoming a debate. Over time, people associate you with ease because they don't feel judged or rushed when they talk to you.

Tip 83: Use Tempo to Regulate the Moment

Tempo is emotional language. If someone is wound up, they usually talk faster. Don't overcorrect with a dramatic slow-down that sounds patronizing. Meet their pace for a beat so they feel understood, then lower your speed slightly on your next response. Small shift, not personality transplant.

Think pace-leading, not pace-policing. Add short pauses after key lines and keep your tone steady enough to follow. A good rule is a ten percent adjustment, not fifty. When you do this well, people start syncing to you without either of you needing to name it, and the conversation gets usable again.

Tip 84: Let Them Arrive First

A lot of people open like they're jumping onto a moving train: straight to the ask, straight to pressure. Efficient, but expensive. A warm start gives the other person one beat to arrive before you hand them the task. You don't need charm school banter. You just need one human line first.

Run this sequence: "How's your day going so far?" Pause, listen, then ask for what you need. Same request, better landing. When the opener is cold, people brace. When it's warm, they collaborate. Do this for one day with every request and you'll feel the difference immediately.

Chapter 36: Reflect Their Strength Back

Everyone walks around with a tiny, invisible mirror held out in front of them. Not literally, obviously. But socially? Absolutely. In the middle of a conversation, while they're nodding and laughing and pretending they're totally chill, part of their brain is still asking: What am I like to you right now? Psychologist Harry Reis has studied something close to the heart of that question, what he calls perceived partner responsiveness.

People feel closer to someone when they sense three things: you get them, you value them, and you're glad they're here, in a grounded, "I actually noticed you" way. This is why some interactions feel easy even when nothing "exciting" happened. You leave feeling steadier because the other person's attention had warmth in it.

A positive projection cue is you making that warmth visible. You casually reveal a good assumption you're holding about them, a quality you've already clocked and genuinely respect. "You've got a calm way of thinking through this." "I like how you ask questions that actually matter." "You always make this less tense." It's small, but it lands big, because it answers that invisible question they were already asking.

This isn't flattery. Flattery has that sticky, needy vibe, like it's trying to buy something. Positive projection is more like turning on a light in a room: it helps people see themselves more clearly, and they usually stand a little taller when the light is kind. They don't feel hyped up. They feel understood in a way that's both specific and unexpectedly relieving.

Tip 85: Turn Respect Into Reflection

Most of us collect positive thoughts about people like we're hoarding good wine for a "special occasion." We notice that a friend is steady under pressure, or a coworker is sharp without being cruel, or someone has a rare talent for making awkward moments less awkward. Then we say nothing. We keep it locked in our head like it doesn't count unless it's delivered in a dramatic toast. Say it out loud instead, but keep it clean.

This works best when it sounds almost casual, like you're stating the weather: "I appreciate how clear you are when things get messy." "You're good at seeing angles I miss." "I like how you don't make this stressful." The key is delivery: one sentence, normal tone, then keep going. Don't hover. Don't follow it with a speech. Don't add "Sorry that was cheesy." Let it land like a fact. A quick way to find one: ask yourself, What do I trust about this person? Name that. People don't just enjoy being praised. They enjoy being accurately recognized.

Tip 86: Name Their Best Version

People usually become the version of themselves they feel is being seen in the room. Call someone unreliable all week and you'll get more guarded behavior. Call out one moment of steadiness, and you'll often get more of that instead.

This isn't fake positivity. It's selective attention. This isn't about inventing a personality for them; you're reinforcing a trait that already showed up. "You handled that calmly." "You asked the right question there." "You kept this from getting messy." Keep it specific and believable. One line is enough.

To practice this, look for one moment today where someone showed a quality you'd like to keep seeing. Name it once, then move on. No speech, no coaching tone. Just a clean signal. People tend to rise toward the role that feels welcomed around them, and that shifts the whole relationship over time.

Section: Bonding & Warmth

Good guidance keeps conversations stable. Warmth is what makes people come back. This section is about the small repeated signals that make you feel safe to return to.

Warmth is built through consistency, not intensity. People trust what feels steady over time.

In this section, the focus is small behaviors with cumulative impact: acknowledgment, follow-through, tone, and memory. Nothing flashy. Just the moves that make people feel safe and valued.

Use these chapters when interactions feel formal, distant, or brittle. Repeated small signals usually do more than one dramatic gesture.

Chapter 37: Ask Better, Go Deeper

You know that feeling when you tell someone a story and they hit you with "Nice" and immediately start talking about themselves? The conversation keeps going, technically, but the air just drops out of it. Most small talk dies this way. Not because people are boring, but because no one hangs around long enough to actually care. Psychologist Todd Kashdan spends a lot of time studying curiosity. His work keeps landing on the same point: curiosity-based questions don't just get more information, they change the emotional quality of the interaction.

When someone asks you what you learned, what surprised you, or how something changed you, your brain switches modes. You stop performing and start reflecting. The conversation moves from "here's what happened" to "here's who I am inside what happened." That is where depth shows up, and where connection actually forms. The curiosity amplifier is simply this: when someone shares something with you, instead of jumping to a new topic, you zoom in. You get fascinated with how their mind worked inside that moment. One good question can make an ordinary story suddenly feel important, not because the event changed, but because the meaning did. Without that zoom-in, conversation turns into headline roulette.

Tip 87: Ask About Meaning, Not Details

Most follow-up questions chase plot. "Then what?" "Where was that?" "Who was there?" Fine, but shallow. Curiosity that amplifies connection goes after interpretation. It sounds like, "What did you take away from that?" or "What stuck with you the most?" or "Did that change how you see things?" That kind of question forces the brain to slow down and sort through experience. People end up revealing what they value, what they fear, what they notice. You get them, not just their schedule. When someone tells you about a trip, a project, or a rough week, skip the logistics.

Ask one question that starts with "What did you…" or "How did that…" and points at their inner world, not the outer events. Then shut up and let them think. The pause might feel slightly heavy for a second. Stay there. That's the moment their answer shifts from automatic to honest.

Tip 88: Stay with One Thread

A lot of people confuse "being interesting" with "covering a lot of ground." So conversations bounce from topic to topic like a playlist on shuffle. You touch ten things and connect on none of them. Curiosity works better like a spotlight than a flashlight. Pick one thread and keep the beam there a little longer than feels natural. When they answer your first curiosity question, don't immediately pivot back to yourself or change lanes.

You can double click once more. "You said that surprised you. In what way?" or "You mentioned that was hard. What part of it was hardest?" It doesn't have to turn into therapy. You're just giving them permission to hear their own thoughts out loud. Watch what happens when you do this in even one conversation. People will often walk away feeling like it was unusually good, even if it only lasted five minutes. They will not say, "Wow, what excellent curiosity techniques." They will think, "I felt weirdly seen." And the funny part is, you didn't become more charming in some abstract way. You just stopped skimming and let your curiosity sit still long enough to actually matter.

You've had this experience: you're telling a story, and someone latches onto one tiny piece of it. Some stories arrive like floating heads. You get the emotion, you get the plot, but you have no idea where any of it is happening or who else is in the frame. "So it was really intense and everything blew up and I just left." Cool. But... where? With who? At work? At brunch? On the moon? Narrative psychologist Jerome Bruner pointed out that humans don't just tell stories, we think in stories. And stories need structure: a setting, a cast, a sense of "where was this?" and "who was there?" Without that map, our brains have to work harder to care.

With it, everything suddenly makes more sense. Details stick, feelings land, and you feel like you were almost there.

The social mapping cue is just a way to add that structure in real time. A couple of small questions can snap the whole scene into focus: "Where were you when this happened?" "Who was there?" "Was this one-on-one or a group situation?" As they answer, the memory sharpens, the emotions get clearer, and they often end up telling a much better story than they thought they had in them. And yes, they'll feel surprisingly good about that, because everyone likes feeling like a compelling version of themselves.

Tip 89: Drop a Pin: Time, Place, People

When someone's talking, notice if their story feels like it's floating. You get the vibe but not the frame.

That's your cue to drop a pin. One tiny mapping question pulls the whole thing into focus. You might ask: "Where were you when that happened?" "Who else was around?" "When was this, roughly?" This tiny move does three useful things. It improves recall, speeds up your understanding, and signals, "I'm actually picturing this with you." That shared map feels surprisingly intimate.

When someone says, "Everything went sideways," don't nod and guess. Ask one grounding question and let the scene come into focus. Their story usually gets clearer, and your connection gets stronger.

People often worry they're rambling or hard to follow. A simple map question helps them feel coherent without making the moment clinical. It's not about directing their story. You're helping it land.

Chapter 38: Make Your Point Easy to Follow

You could feel it when someone talks in a way your brain doesn't want to follow. Long, winding sentences, stacked clauses, niche jargon, ten ideas in one breath. Your eyes stay polite, but inside you're quietly tapping the "skip" button. It's rarely that the person is wrong. It's that listening to them feels like carrying groceries up four flights of stairs. Possible, sure. Enjoyable? No. And here's the annoying part: even if what they're saying is brilliant, the effort required to decode it makes them seem less brilliant. Not fair, but that's the human brain for you. We judge the message and the messenger based on how hard the message is to process.

Princeton psychologist Daniel Oppenheimer studied this and found that when information is easier to process, people tend to rate it as more intelligent, more trustworthy, and more likable. In other words, clarity often reads as competence. Which is a problem, because a lot of us were trained to do the opposite. We learned to "sound smart," add extra qualifiers, stack details, and lace our sentences with complexity like we're getting paid by the clause.

Meanwhile the listener is out here trying to survive their inbox, their commute, and whatever is happening with their lower back. The cognitive ease bridge makes conversation feel like a ramp instead of a wall. Start with plain language and short sentences, especially when introducing a new idea, opinion, or request. Give the one-line version first, then add detail only if needed.

This isn't "dumbing down." It's respect for attention. Most people are running on limited bandwidth. Clear delivery helps them meet you faster, respond more thoughtfully, and engage the meaning instead of wrestling with the wording.

Tip 90: Lead with the One-Sentence Version

Most conversations get confusing because we lead with the long version. Your brain has context, caveats, and side notes. The other person has none of that yet. Give them the headline first.

Think: one sentence that tells them what this is actually about. "My main concern is timing." "Short version: I want us to simplify this." "Bottom line: I'd like us to talk more directly." Then, if needed, add detail.

This tiny move changes everything. People stop guessing your point and start engaging with it. They ask better questions. You sound clearer without sounding rigid.

Quick rep: before any high-stakes conversation, force yourself to write the one-sentence version first. If you can't state it cleanly, you're probably not ready for the long version either. Lead with the headline, then expand only as needed.

Tip 91: Save Complexity for Later

There's nothing wrong with detail. The problem is timing. When you front-load complexity, people mentally bail before you get to the point. When you earn their attention with clarity first, the same level of detail suddenly feels interesting instead of heavy. One practical route is to literally ask for permission to go deeper. "Do you want the quick version or the nerdy version?" "I can give you the simple take, then the nuance if you want it." If they opt in, their brain is already leaning forward.

That's cognitive ease doing its job: they know where this is going, so extra information has somewhere to land. Pay attention in your next conversation: if someone's eyes glaze a little or they stop tracking, don't assume they're rude. Ask yourself, "Did I make this easy enough to follow before I made it detailed?" Then trim your next sentence in half. The more you practice that, the more people start describing you as "clear," "easy to talk to," and "calm," even if your ideas are huge and messy behind the scenes. You didn't get simpler. You just learned how to build a bridge instead of dropping a bookshelf on them.

Chapter 39: Pull Forward the Good

There's a huge difference between, "How are you?" and "Anything good happen today?" The first one usually gets you a reflex answer: "Fine, busy, tired, same as always." Autopilot. The second forces a tiny search. Even on a rough day, the brain goes, Was there anything good? That little search is where the magic lives. Psychologist Barbara Fredrickson, who studies positive emotions, suggests that recalling good moments doesn't just feel nice in theory. It literally shifts mood, increases openness, and makes people more flexible and generous in how they think. Remembering something pleasant isn't neutral; it nudges the emotional thermostat upward. When you ask someone about a good moment from their day or week, you're not being fluffy.

You're steering the emotional tone of the conversation toward warmth, without ignoring reality.

So ask for the bright spot. It's a small question with a big mood shift like, "What's something good that happened today?" or "What's been a bright spot this week?" You're not asking them to deny stress or pain. You're just shining a brief light somewhere that doesn't hurt. And very often, that light spills over into how the rest of the interaction feels.

Tip 92: Ask for One Bright Spot

People freeze up if you ask them to pretend everything's great. "How's life?" can feel overwhelming. "What's something good that happened today?" is smaller, kinder, and easier to answer honestly. It doesn't erase their struggles. It just makes room for something else to exist alongside them. When you're checking in with a friend, partner, or coworker, swap out the standard "How are you?" for something like: "What's one good thing that's happened so far today?" "Anything even slightly not-terrible about this week?" Say it lightly, with a half-smile if it fits. You're giving them permission to remember that their day wasn't only stress. And if they say, "Honestly?

Not much," you can always respond with, "Fair, it's been a lot," and stay with them there. This isn't forced positivity. It's opening a door that might lead somewhere softer.

Tip 93: Let the Good Moment Breathe

When someone does share something good, the temptation is to immediately jump in with your own story. "Oh, you got good feedback? Me too, my boss said..." And just like that, the moment turns into a subtle competition instead of shared enjoyment. A better move is to stay with their good thing for one more beat. "That's awesome. What did you like most about that?" "Nice. How did that make the rest of your day feel?"

You're helping them savor it instead of rushing past it. That extra ten seconds of attention turns a throwaway positive note into something that actually shifts their emotional state. Here's a simple rule: when someone shares a win, give their win one extra lap before you bring yours in. Or not at all. You'll notice the conversation feels warmer, lighter, and oddly more connected, even if you only talked for a few minutes. You didn't "cheer them up." You just helped them stand a little longer in a part of their day that didn't suck. And people remember how that feels.

Chapter 40: Reset Before It Drifts

You could be five minutes into a conversation, nodding, talking, agreeing, and still not be talking about the same thing. It's like you're both using the word "trip," but one of you means "weekend in Paris" and the other means "fell down the stairs." Feels fine… until it doesn't. Philosopher and language nerd Paul Grice spent a lot of time looking at how we assume shared understanding in conversation. His work highlighted a simple problem: we think we're on the same page way more often than we actually are. When the invisible pages don't match, confusion builds quietly, then leaks out as annoyance, shutdown, or weird vibes neither person can quite name.

A quick tune-up here saves a lot of weirdness later. It's one short question that asks, "Are we actually talking about the same thing right now?" Not in a dramatic, "We need to talk" way, but as a quick tune-up. "Are we thinking about this the same way?" "Just to check, is this what you mean?" That little adjustment can save you from ten minutes of talking past each other and two hours of wondering why it felt strange.

Tip 94: Call a Time-Out Early

No need to wait for a full derailment before you reset the conversation. The best time to pause is when things start feeling slightly off, not when both of you are already annoyed.

Watch for early signs: you're answering a question they didn't ask, they're reacting to a point you didn't make, or both of you keep repeating the same words with different meanings. That's your cue.

Use a quick calibration line: "Can I check that we're talking about the same thing?" or "Let me make sure I have your point right." Then offer your plain-language summary and let them correct it.

If they say yes, great - momentum returns. If they say no, even better - now you're fixing the real issue instead of fighting a phantom version of it. This habit saves more conversations than brilliant arguments ever will.

Tip 95: Treat "Not Quite" as a Win

A lot of people avoid checking in because they're scared of hearing, "No, that's not what I meant." It feels like getting something wrong in class. In reality, that's the best possible answer. It means you just caught a misunderstanding while it was still small. When someone corrects you, don't tense up or rush to defend your interpretation. You can simply say, "Got it, thanks for clarifying," and offer a shorter, updated version: "Okay, so you're more worried about timing than the actual plan." "So it's not the project, it's how it was handled." Now you're both looking at the same thing. Same page, same paragraph.

The emotional temperature usually drops right there, because people feel relieved to finally be accurately understood. What you can do is reframe calibration in your head as maintenance instead of criticism. You're not being "picky" by asking if you're on the same page. You're preventing both of you from wasting time on parallel monologues.

People start giving you clearer answers because you keep the conversation on one track.

Chapter 41: Find the Shared Thread

There's a tiny "oh thank God" moment that happens when someone says, "Wait, you're into that too?" It could be running, horror movies, Korean dramas, tabletop games, powerlifting, weird productivity apps, whatever. For half a second, the air changes. You're no longer two separate planets. There's at least one shared continent. Psychologist Donn Byrne spent years studying what's called the similarity–attraction effect, and the result is pretty simple: the more overlap people perceive, the more they like each other.

It's not just, "We both enjoy this thing." The brain cheats and goes, If we share this, we probably share other things too. Values. Humor. Vibe. Even if that's not always true, the feeling is real, and the feeling is what matters in the moment. The shared interest finder is about catching those overlaps in real time and saying something instead of just feeling a spark and moving on. When someone mentions something that genuinely lights you up too, you flag it: "I love that too. What got you into it?" One line. Now the conversation isn't just two monologues. It's two stories braided around something you both care about.

Tip 96: Mark the Moment of "Me Too"

Many people let the "oh cool, same" moment slip by quietly. They smile, they feel the click, and then they change the subject. Which is tragic, because that's the easiest opening you'll ever get for real connection. When you next feel that jolt of overlap, don't keep it in your head. Say it out loud, but keep it light and focused on them: "I'm into that too. What pulled you into it?"

"Same here. When did you start?" "I love that stuff. What's your favorite part of it?" Notice what you're doing there: you're naming the similarity, then immediately tossing the ball back. You're not launching into a five-minute TED Talk about your obsession.

You're saying, "We have this in common, and I want to hear your version." That's flattering, disarming, and weirdly rare. To build fluency in one conversation, catch exactly one "me too" moment and mark it with a sentence plus a question. See how quickly the energy shifts from polite to easy.

Tip 97: Let Shared Interests Open Doors

The risk with shared interests is turning them into a brag-off. You both like the same band, and suddenly it's a trivia contest about obscure B-sides. That doesn't build closeness. It builds quiet resentment and a desire to fake a phone call. Use the overlap as a door, not a stage. After you've both said, "Oh, you too?", steer toward meaning instead of stats. "What do you like most about it?" "Has it changed anything for you?" "Is there a story behind how you got into it?" Now you're not just bonding over a thing. You're bonding over what that thing says about each of you. That's where people reveal their personality, not just their preferences.

Pay attention to how it feels when you handle it this way. The conversation usually relaxes. You stop trying to prove you belong in the fan club and start enjoying that you're in good company. And long after you forget exactly what you talked about, both of you will remember one simple feeling: "We're kind of the

same, at least in one way that matters to us." That's
more than enough to build on.

Chapter 42: Use Tiny Stories

A clean way to do it is to tell a lot about someone from the way they say, "That reminds me of this one time..." Not the epic vacation recaps or the 45–minute career saga. The tiny stuff. The three–sentence memory about a teacher, a weird first job, a strange Uber ride, the time they panicked in a grocery store aisle. Those little stories are where personality leaks out. Narrative psychologist Dan McAdams talks about how we build our identity out of small stories we tell about ourselves.

Not just what happened, but what it meant to us. When you share a micro-story in conversation, you're handing someone a puzzle piece of who you are. You're saying, "Here's how my brain works. Here's what I notice. Here's what I find funny, annoying, beautiful, or terrifying." It's fast, it's light, and it's way more effective than generic facts like "I like movies" or "I'm into fitness."

Drop a small story that fits the moment, then hand it back. Instead of just agreeing or nodding, you toss in a tiny, specific moment from your own life that connects to what they said. Not to steal the spotlight, but to make the conversation more vivid, more human, and more fun.

Tip 98: Trade One Fact for One Scene

Labels are efficient, but they're forgettable. "I'm into fitness." "I love traveling." "I'm a creative person." None of that gives people much to hold.

A tiny scene does. "I signed up for a 6 a.m. class and immediately regretted all my life choices." "I once got lost in Lisbon and found my favorite cafe by accident." Same idea, but now it's alive.

Run this quick check, rule: when you're about to state a trait, swap it for one short moment that shows the trait in action. Keep it under four sentences. No TED Talk. No moral at the end.

People remember scenes because scenes have texture. They can picture them. So if you want your point to stick, give one concrete moment, then move on. Small story, big memory.

Tip 99: Use Micro-Stories as Invitations

There's a fine line between sparking connection and turning the whole interaction into The You Show. Micro-stories work best when they feel like a hand extended, not a spotlight grabbed. The difference is what you do after you tell it. A good rhythm looks like this: They share something → you drop a short, identity–revealing story → you toss the ball back. For example: "That reminds me of when I tried that and totally froze in front of everyone. I realized I hate being put on the spot. Is it like that for you too, or do you kind of enjoy the pressure?" See what happened there? You revealed something real, then immediately made it about both of you again.

That makes the story feel like an invitation to connect, not a monologue you're forcing them to sit through. In your next decent conversation, share one micro-story, then follow it with a curious question that lets them respond with their own version. You'll feel the interaction click from "information exchange" into something warmer and more alive. You didn't overshare. You just gave them a tiny, honest glimpse of who's sitting in front of them and invited them to do the same.

Chapter 43: Praise the Process, Not Just the Outcome

There's a specific kind of sting that comes from being praised the wrong way. You finish something hard. Someone says, "Wow, you make it look easy." And you smile, because you're polite, but inside you're thinking: cool, love being congratulated for my ability to suffer quietly.

Carol Dweck's research on praise gets at why this matters. When people are praised for outcomes or fixed traits ("You're so talented"), they get more fragile. They start protecting the identity. They avoid challenges that might mess up the label. But when praise points to effort, strategy, or persistence, people become more willing to take on difficult things. They feel recognized for the part that actually carried them. Adults are not immune to this. We just hide it better. We still want someone to notice the late-night draft, the practice reps, the decision to keep going when quitting would've been easier.

The effort highlight cue is a small shift in what you choose to applaud. The result matters, sure, but the work underneath is where people live. When you name that work, your compliment stops being decoration and starts being fuel.

Tip 100: Applaud the How, Not Just Wow

Quick, shallow praise sounds nice, but it dies fast. "You won, good job." "That's awesome, you're talented." It bounces off because it sticks to the surface. Effort-based acknowledgment goes deeper. It validates the part of them that showed up, struggled, and chose not to quit.

You can swap a lot of your standard compliments with minor rewrites: instead of "You're so good at this," try "You've clearly put a lot of time into getting good at this." Instead of "That presentation was perfect," try "You structured that so clearly, it's obvious you prepared carefully." Instead of "You always handle things so well," try "I notice how you stay with hard things instead of checking out."

Pick one person today and aim all your praise at what they did, not who they're "supposed" to be. Watch their reaction. People don't just smile, they soften. Being seen for effort feels like relief. It says, "I know this didn't just fall out of you. I see the grind."

Most compliments show up at the finish line. That's fine. The real power move is noticing effort mid-journey, when the outcome isn't guaranteed.

Chapter 44: Set the Frame Before the Ask

"Can we talk?" That sentence has ruined more afternoons than traffic. Your brain immediately opens the worst-case-scenario folder. Am I in trouble? Is this about work? That text I forgot to answer? My browser history? When the frame is missing, your nervous system fills it in with whatever horror movie it has in stock.

Sociologist Erving Goffman spent years studying how people manage impressions and interactions. One of his big insights was that conversations feel safer when the situation is clearly framed. In other words, people relax when they know what kind of moment they're in. A tiny preview like, "Can we spend a minute on the meeting from earlier?" or "I wanted to ask you something about that project," gives the interaction walls and a floor.

The micro-agenda check is a small framing move that keeps things focused and respectful. Before diving into your point, you give a one-line heads-up about what you want to talk about and roughly how big it is. It sounds almost too simple to matter, but that one sentence can lower defensiveness, prevent spirals, and stop conversations from feeling like surprise audits.

Tip 101: Frame the Talk, Lower the Heat

A lot of awkward conversations aren't failing because of content. They're failing because nobody knows the frame. Are we venting, brainstorming, deciding, or just checking in?

Set the frame early and people relax fast. "Can I vent for two minutes, then get your take?" "Quick tactical question, not a deep dive." "This is sensitive, so I want to go slow." One line like that prevents ten minutes of mismatch.

You could frame time, depth, role, or tone. You don't need all four. Pick one that matters in the moment and keep moving.

This isn't corporate scripting. It's social clarity. You're telling the other person what lane you're in so they can meet you there. And when people know the lane, they stop bracing and start participating.

Chapter 45: Name Their Signature Strength

Everyone has a few things they quietly know they're good at. Not the résumé stuff, the deeper things. Being steady in a crisis. Seeing patterns. Making people laugh without trying. Asking sharp questions. You probably have a couple of these "that's just me" qualities. You also probably don't hear them named out loud very often. Psychologist Martin Seligman has done a ton of work on what he calls "signature strengths," those natural traits people feel most aligned with. When someone recognizes those strengths, people don't just feel flattered. They feel understood. They think, "Yes, that's me," and instantly feel safer and more connected to the person who noticed.

This is why a simple line like "You have a calm way of breaking things down" can feel oddly moving. It is accurate, specific, and aimed right at the story they hold about themselves. That's the signature strength mirror: you spot a natural strength in someone, then reflect it back in a clean, grounded sentence. Not over the top, not poetic, just precise. "You always bring good structure to conversations." "You're great at making people feel included." "You have a talent for finding the angle everyone else missed." When you do that well, you're not just handing out compliments. You are handing people a clearer version of themselves, and they will remember who held that mirror up.

Tip 102: Name Strength in Everyday Language

The temptation is to go too big. "You're incredible." "You're a genius." "You're such a leader." Those are nice, but they are so broad they often bounce off. A signature strength mirror works best when it is specific and casual, almost like an observation you are saying in passing. Watch how someone naturally shows up in conversations. Do they slow things down when everyone else is spiraling. Do they organize messy ideas. Do they bring playfulness at exactly the right moment. Once you spot a pattern, describe it in simple language tied to a real situation.

"I notice you have a calming effect when everyone else gets stressed." "You always find a clean way to organize messy thoughts." "You're really good at spotting angles other people miss." You're not inventing a personality for them. You are labeling something they already do, which is why it lands so deeply. Pick one person in your life and spend a day quietly watching for a repeat strength. When you see it, put it into one sentence and say it once. Then let it sit. No big speech required.

Tip 103: Mirror the Story They Tell Themselves

This cue hits hardest when what you say matches how they secretly hope to see themselves. People want others to view them in a way that fits their own inner narrative. When that lines up, there is a little click you can almost feel. When it doesn't, it can feel flattering but slightly off, like trying on a shirt that is almost your size. To get that alignment, pay attention to how they talk about themselves or what they are proud of. Do they light up when they talk about helping others. Do they mention loving systems, fairness, creativity, humor. Those are clues. When you reflect a strength, aim close to that territory.

With the helper: "You have a real gift for making people feel taken care of." With the systems person: "You bring structure to chaos in such a natural way." With the creative one: "You always come at things from a fresh angle, it changes the conversation." After you say it, resist the urge to immediately pivot or downplay it with a joke. Give them a second to absorb it. Often you will see a tiny shift in their expression, like something inside just relaxed or stood up a bit straighter. That's the feeling of being seen, not just praised. And people tend to stay close to the ones who see them in a way that feels true.

Chapter 46: Point to the Next Moment

Some conversations end like a phone dying at 3 percent. Not dramatic, just… gone. "Cool, yeah, anyway… I should go." You both drift away, and the whole thing disappears from memory like a browser tab you accidentally closed. Nothing wrong happened, there's just no sense that this moment connects to anything later. It lives and dies in the same ten minutes. Relationship researchers like John Caughlin have found that forward-oriented statements, even tiny ones, increase feelings of closeness. When you say things like "On your next rep, you have to tell me more about that," or "I want to hear how that turns out," you're not making a huge promise.

You are planting a small flag in the future that says, "I expect you to still be in my world." That hint of continuity changes how the present moment feels. It goes from a one-off interaction to one chapter in an ongoing story. That's the shared future cue. It's one simple line that points past the current conversation: something you want to revisit, hear more about, or do together. It is subtle, but it does a lot at once. It signals interest, emotional investment, and an assumption that this connection is not disposable. People pick up on that, even if they never name it out loud.

Tip 104: Tag One Thread for Later

Think of every good conversation as throwing out a few possible "bookmarks." A project they are working on. A trip they are planning. A fear they are wrestling with. An idea they're excited about. The shared future cue is just choosing one of those threads and saying, "I want to see where that goes." For example: "Next time we talk, I want an update on that." "You have to tell me how that turns out." "I'm curious where you'll land with that decision. Let me know." You're not scheduling anything formal. You're just marking something as important enough to remember. That alone makes people feel valued. Their life is not just noise you listened to politely.

It's something you plan to come back to. In your next conversation, as you feel a conversation wrapping up, quickly scan for one thing they mentioned that has a "to be continued" baked in. Then drop a single forward-facing line about it before you say goodbye. Short, light, genuine. You'll notice the goodbye feels warmer, less like a door closing and more like a page turning.

Tip 105: Hint: You're Still on My Map

A lot of rapport dies between conversations, not during them. You have a good interaction, then silence, then both people reset to zero next time.

The fix is tiny: leave one line that implies continuity. "Tell me how that goes next week." "Remind me to ask you about that class." "I want the update when you hear back." You're quietly saying, "You still exist on my map after this ends."

Then do the second half: actually follow up. One short ping later - "How'd it go?" - is worth more than a polished goodbye in the moment.

It doesn't need to be constant. It needs to be real. A few clean continuity cues turn you from "nice to talk to" into "actually remembers me," and people feel that difference immediately.

Chapter 47: Open Without Awkwardness

Cold starts are where social confidence goes to die. You see someone you could talk to at a coffee shop, networking event, hallway, or school pickup, and your brain suddenly forgets every normal sentence you have ever spoken. You reach for the classic "So, what do you do?" or "How's it going?" and immediately feel like a glitchy NPC. Conversation analyst Elizabeth Stokoe has spent years studying how real people actually start interactions, not in theory, but in recorded calls and conversations. One of her big findings is that openers that notice something rather than demand something create less friction.

An opener like "It's really busy in here today," or "They always play good music at this place," gives the other person an easy runway. They can respond if they want, or just smile and let it float. No pressure, no quiz. So skip the question and drop an observation. "This place has such good energy today." "That's a strong notebook game you've got going there." "They really cranked the AC in here." It's a small comment that opens the door without shoving anyone through it. If they engage, great. If they don't, you haven't cornered them. And in a world full of forced small talk and hard pivots, that soft, optional start feels like a relief.

Tip 106: Start with "I Notice"

Questions put people on the spot, especially early on. "Where are you from?" "What do you do?" "Why are you here?" Those all require decisions, self-presentation, and tiny micro-calculations. An observation just joins them in the moment they're already in. It's more like standing next to them at a window and pointing out the view. A simple move is to build a whole repertoire of low-pressure openers by focusing on three things you can always notice: Environment: "This place is louder than I expected." "They always have the best coffee smell in here." Shared situation: "We picked the right line.

That one hasn't moved." "This meeting room is freezing." Neutral props: "That's a great mug." "Those are very organized notes." Say it with a light tone, almost like you're thinking out loud. If they want to play, they will pick it up. If they are not in the mood, you haven't cornered them with a question they feel rude ignoring. One small observation, then let the moment breathe.

Tip 107: Let the Conversation Grow Naturally

The whole point of an effortless opener is that it does not try to do too much. You don't need to immediately stack more lines or scramble for the follow-up. Your next move can simply build on however they respond. If they give you a short answer plus a little extra, you can gently follow that thread: Them: "Yeah, it is busy. It's always like this on Fridays." You: "You come here a lot on Fridays?" If they just smile or nod, that's still useful information. They might be shy, tired, or just done with talking. You can respect that by not pushing. Maybe you add one more tiny comment, then turn back to what you were doing.

You still come across as warm, not awkward. Try treating effortless openers as tiny invitations, not contracts. Your job is to toss one light line into the space, then read the response. If the spark catches, you build slowly from what they give you. If it doesn't, no problem. You practiced being open without being intrusive, which is its own kind of social confidence. With practice, you'll notice your fear of "starting conversations" shrinking, because you're no longer starting with pressure. You're starting with presence.

Section: Repair & Tension

Warmth does not remove friction. It just gives you enough trust to repair it. This section is about what to do when things wobble so the relationship does not pay for one rough moment.

Tension isn't a failure. Avoidance usually is.

This section helps you handle friction without escalation, withdrawal, or overcorrection. The emphasis is acknowledgment, pacing, and repair language that keeps dignity intact for both people.

If conversations feel brittle, reactive, or easily derailed, start here. The aim is not perfect harmony. It's resilient dialogue that can survive real disagreement.

Chapter 48: Reset the Rhythm

You could feel it when a conversation starts sprinting. Words pile on words, both of you are talking quickly, interrupting slightly, stacking half-finished thoughts. Nobody is really breathing. You walk away wired, not connected. It feels like you were juggling instead of relating. Studies on cognitive load and processing speed keep pointing to the same thing: when the pace slows down even a little, people think more clearly and feel more at ease. Fast talk is great for brainstorming or banter. But deeper, more personal things tend to come out at a calmer tempo. Slowing your voice a notch gives both brains more bandwidth. It reduces the sense of performance and turns the interaction from "keep up" into "be here."

That's the rhythm reset. When a moment starts to feel rushed, tense, or slightly out of control, you dial your own pace down just a bit. Not into sleepy territory, just a softer gear. You let a beat exist between sentences. You pause before responding. You breathe. Conversation shifts from a race to a walk. And walking is where people start saying the real stuff.

Tip 108: Use Your Pace as a Brake

When things speed up, the instinct is to match it. They talk faster, you talk faster, and now you are both driving 90 on a road that should be 45. Instead of matching, you can become the brake. Not by telling them to calm down, but by quietly changing how you speak. For a clean rep, try this when a conversation feels rushed: drop your volume just slightly, stretch your sentences out with small pauses, and take one visible breath before you answer a loaded question. For example: "Okay… give me a second to think about that." "Right… so here's what stands out to me." Your nervous system will want to speed back up.

Let it complain while your voice stays slow. Often, the other person's pace will start syncing with yours without either of you mentioning it. You just reset the rhythm by refusing to sprint.

Tip 109: Create Space with Tiny Pauses

Depth usually doesn't come from smarter questions. It comes from slower rhythm. If every pause gets filled instantly, people stay on the safe, fast version of what they mean.

Give this a quick rep today: after someone says something that clearly matters, wait one extra beat before replying. Not dramatic silence. Just enough space for the thought to settle. If helpful, you can lightly mark it: "Give me a second, I'm with you." Then stay quiet.

That small pause does two useful things. It shows you're actually processing, and it gives them room to continue if they're not done yet. A lot of "what I really meant" moments happen in that tiny gap.

You don't need to slow every conversation to a crawl. Just lower the tempo when the moment gets real. That's usually where the better conversation starts.

Chapter 49: Rewind to the Turning Point

Every good story has a moment you wish the person would linger on. They blow past the interesting part, then camp on the boring summary. "I was freaking out, and then it all worked out somehow." Somehow? No. Absolutely not. That's the part we want. Narrative psychology folks have found that when people "rewind" a story and walk back through a key moment, they access richer detail, more emotion, and clearer meaning. When you invite someone to back up a bit, you're not being picky, you're helping their brain reopen the file. Details come back. Feelings come into focus. The story gets better, and the connection between you deepens. That's the curious rewind.

You hear something interesting fly by, then gently hit the conversational rewind button. "Wait, go back for a second, what happened right before that?" or "Hold on, you said you almost quit, what led up to that?" It's a small question with a big signal underneath it: I'm not just tolerating your story. I'm invested enough to want the good parts in high resolution. Done well, this does two things at once. It helps them tell a better story, and it helps them touch memories that feel more alive, often more positive or more meaningful. The tone of the conversation shifts from casual recap to shared scene. You're not just catching up anymore.

You are standing in the moment with them.

Tip 110: Rewind to the Moment Before

Whenever someone says something like "And then it all changed," or "Suddenly I realized," your ears should perk up. Those transition lines are usually sitting on top of a moment they have not fully told you about. The curious rewind goes after that hidden scene. One practical route is to jump in lightly with: "Wait, back up, what was happening right before you decided that?" "Go back a bit, what pushed you to that point?" "Hold on, when you say you were freaking out, what was actually going through your head?" You're not interrogating them, you are spotlighting the hinge of the story. As they rewind, they often remember more than they thought they would.

Faces, rooms, small details, the exact sentence someone said. That extra texture pulls you in and, just as importantly, helps them understand their own experience more clearly. As a practice drill in your next real conversation, when someone hits a "and then everything changed" type line, don't nod and move on. Ask for the moment right before it. One rewind, one focused question. Watch how the story deepens without you needing any profound insight. You just refused to let the good part stay blurry.

Tip 111: Rewind Toward What Lights Them Up

Rewinding is not just for heavy or dramatic moments. It's also perfect for the parts that make people quietly glow. When someone mentions something they clearly enjoy, then rushes past it, you can pull the timeline back to let them enjoy it a bit longer. That alone can lift the whole emotional tone of the conversation. Listen for sparks.

A hobby they "love," a trip that was "amazing," a project that was "actually really fun." Instead of saying, "Nice," and changing the topic, try saying: "Wait, that sounds great, what was your favorite part right before that?" "Go back, what set that whole thing in motion?" "Back up a bit, when did you realize you were really into that?" You're guiding them toward memories that feel good to revisit. That creates an upward pull for both of you. They get to relive something meaningful, you get to see them in their element, and the vibe of the conversation tilts toward curiosity and warmth instead of routine checking in.

As a small experiment, pick one person and decide you are going to use one curious rewind with them in the next few days, aimed specifically at something that excites them. When they mention it, stop the timeline and invite them back into that moment. Very often you will see their energy rise, their body relax, and their story get sharper. That is storytelling chemistry, and you helped create it with one simple, well placed "Wait, go back."

Chapter 50: Interrupt to Appreciate

Most of us treat interruptions like social toxins. You're taught to wait your turn, never cut in, let people finish. Which is good, mostly. But not all interruptions land the same way. There's a difference between hijacking the mic and jumping in just to say, "Wait, that was really good." One shuts people down. The other makes them feel like they just hit a nerve in the best way. Studies on interpersonal warmth and "positive affect bursts" show that small, unexpected moments of praise or enthusiasm give relationships a boost. When you cut in only to appreciate someone, you are breaking the rhythm in a way that signals, "What you just said matters enough to stop everything for a second."

A line like, "Hold on. That's actually such a good point," is disarming. They were braced for being corrected or talked over. Instead, you catch their idea, raise it in the air, and say, "Look at this." An appreciation interruption is the polite version of tapping the brakes. You pause the flow for one beat to underline what they just said, then you hand the mic right back. Done right, it feels like a spotlight and a hug at the same time. Interruptions are not always rude. Some are small celebrations.

Tip 112: Interrupt Only to Elevate

The difference between an annoying interruption and a warm one is intent. Bad interruptions grab the wheel. Good ones hit pause to admire the view. You're not jumping in to change the topic or one-up them. You're jumping in to say, "Stop, that was really good, and I don't want it to get lost." You could keep it simple: "Hold up, that's such a sharp way to put it."

"Wait, that's actually a really helpful point." "Can we just appreciate that for a second, that's so well said." Then, crucially, you give the floor back. You don't launch into a five-minute speech about your own brilliance.

You might add, "Please keep going," or, "I just didn't want that to slide by." The interruption becomes a little frame around their idea, not a doorway into your monologue. Use this short test, in your next real conversation, listen for one moment where they say something thoughtful, honest, or brave. Instead of just silently admiring it, interrupt gently and name it. One sentence, then hand the conversation back. Watch how their face shifts. Most people are starving for that kind of in-the-moment recognition.

Tip 113: Anchor Emotion Mid-Conversation

A quick appreciation in the middle of a hard conversation can calm the room faster than another explanation. Not a big speech. Just one clean line that marks what is working.

"I appreciate how directly you're saying this." "Thanks for sticking with this even though it's awkward." "I can feel you're trying to solve it, not win it."

Then keep moving. That part matters. If you overdo it, it sounds manipulative. If you keep it brief and specific, it feels like respect.

Use this when tension is rising but both people are still trying. You're giving the conversation a small emotional anchor so it doesn't slide into pure defensiveness. Sometimes one sentence is enough to stop the spiral and bring both people back to the actual issue.

Chapter 51: Show There's Time

Nothing kills a story faster than feeling like the other person is on a timer. You can sense it instantly. The quick glances at the door, the "uh-huh, uh-huh" while they mentally sprint ahead, the vibe of "Can you land this plane already." Your mouth keeps talking, but some deeper part of you quietly shuts the door. Studies on time perception and trust keep finding the same pattern: when people feel like there's enough time, they open up more and feel safer. When everything feels rushed, the brain moves into efficiency mode, not honesty mode. Relaxed pacing tells the nervous system, "We're not under threat right now." That makes vulnerability and clarity much more likely.

In human terms, the person who makes you feel like you don't have to race is the person you end up telling the real story to. That's the conversational patience signal. It's any small way you show, "I'm not in a hurry, I'm here with you." A simple "Take your time" while they're thinking, or "I'm not going anywhere, go ahead," can change the whole tone of an interaction. A one-second pause is basically conversational elbow room. People stop scrambling and start actually answering. Rushed listening makes everyone sound like they're narrating an evacuation.

Tip 114: Say There's No Rush

People often assume you're busy, even when you're not. They've learned, usually the hard way, that most listeners have short attention spans and overloaded calendars. So they compress their stories and skip the parts that actually matter. A simple patience signal interrupts that old script. When they pause to think, instead of jumping in, try saying: "Take your time, I'm listening." "I'm in no rush, say it how you need to." "It's okay if it takes a second to find the words." You're not overreacting. Their nervous system just heard "safe" instead of "threat." Slow down. Take a breath. Let the moment land.

To build fluency in your next deeper conversation, any time they stall, look away to think, or say "I'm not sure how to explain this," resist the temptation to rescue the silence. Offer one short line that explicitly says there's time. Then stay quiet. You'll often see their shoulders drop a little and their answer get more real, because they're no longer editing for speed.

Tip 115: Let Your Body Prove It

Words help, but your body will rat you out if it's not on the same page. You can say "Take your time" and completely ruin it by glancing at your phone, fidgeting, or half-standing like you're about to bolt. Patience has to show up in your posture, your gestures, even the environment you create. A few simple ways to dial up comfort and relaxation: Remove obvious time pressure. Flip your phone face down. Stop checking the clock every two minutes. If you really do have a limit, name it early: "I've got ten minutes, but they're yours." Clear beats secret rushing. Use open, unhurried body language. Lean back a little instead of hovering on the edge of your seat.

Uncross your arms. Let your hands rest instead of drumming them. Look at them, not over their shoulder. Your body should feel like a chair they can sit their thoughts in, not a bus that's about to pull away. Let silence be part of the rhythm. When they stop talking, count to two in your head before you respond. If they're searching for words, don't trample the moment with nervous chatter. Your calmness gives them permission to think. What you're really saying underneath all of this is, "You're not an interruption."

That message lowers pressure instantly and helps people stay open long enough to say what they actually mean.

Chapter 52: Ask for One Wow

Some conversations stay stuck at ground level. Schedules, complaints, logistics, the eternal "yeah, things are busy." Necessary, but not exactly soul food. Then someone says, "I saw this thing the other day that absolutely blew my mind," and you can feel the air change. People lean in for that.

Our brains love a little awe. Psychologist Dacher Keltner's research suggests that awe doesn't just feel nice, it can make people more open, generous, and socially warm. A sunset, a concert, a random act of kindness, a wild coincidence, even a brilliant paragraph can do it. Those moments pull us out of cramped, self-focused thinking and into a wider headspace.

That's what the shared-wonder prompt uses. Instead of "How are you?" for the thousandth time, try "What's something that amazed you recently?" or "Have you seen anything lately that made you go wow?" It's not therapy and not an interview. It's just a better doorway. When people take it, the conversation gets more vivid and way more memorable.

Tip 116: Ask for One Small "Wow"

People freeze if you make the prompt feel too grand. If you say, "What's the most awe-inspiring experience of your life?", half of them will panic and mentally scroll through every year since childhood. Too big. The magic is in making the question small and current. One recent moment. One tiny wow. A clean way to do it is to keep it casual: "What's something that surprised you in a good way lately?" "Seen or heard anything recently that made you go, 'Wait, that's wild'?" "Any tiny thing this week that made you think, 'Huh, that's pretty cool'?" Then let them pick the scale.

It might be a huge trip, or it might be the way the light hit an old building at 5 p.m. Both are fair game. There isn't a "good" answer, just a real one. Once they start describing it, the conversation gets texture and feeling, and you learn what actually flips their brain into "alive." Way better than "Yeah, work's fine." Pick one person in your life and swap out your default opener for a wonder-based one. One question, one pause. Instead of a status report, you'll actually get a story.

Tip 117: Stay Inside Their Wonder

When someone shares a moment of genuine wonder, don't rush to summarize it or turn it into advice. Stay with it for one beat longer than feels efficient.

Ask one question that keeps the light on that moment: "What surprised you most?" "What about that stayed with you?" "Why do you think that hit you so hard?" Then listen.

The temptation is to pivot quickly to your own story or to the practical takeaway. Resist that once. Let them sit inside their own meaning first.

This is one of those subtle social moves that changes everything. People feel less handled and more understood. And strangely, the practical insight usually gets better when you don't rush to extract it.

Practice it once today where the stakes are low. If the conversation loosens quickly, the habit is sticking.

Chapter 53: Make a Playful Guess

There's a special glint people get in their eyes when they're about to deliver the twist in a story. You can feel it. They start building up the scene, laying out the cast, hinting that something went sideways. Most listeners sit there politely, waiting for the punchline to arrive. A more fun move is to lean in and say, "I'm guessing this took a turn?" Research on conversational storytelling suggests that listeners who make little predictive comments, like "Let me guess, they showed up late," or "I have a feeling I know where this is going," pull the teller in more. The story stops being a solo performance and becomes a shared project. The brain likes that.

It shifts from passive reception to active play. Even if your prediction is wrong, the signal underneath it is flattering: I'm engaged enough to care what happens next. That's the playful prediction move. You're not spoiling the story. You're poking it with a smile. "I'm betting this did not go how you planned," or "I feel like there's a plot twist coming." Used lightly, it adds energy to the moment, keeps the teller talking, and makes them feel like they are telling this to someone who's actually in the scene with them, not just being polite.

Tip 118: Drop a Soft Guess

Predictions work best when they're gentle and slightly underconfident. Think: friendly nudge, not courtroom objection. The aim is to reflect the tension you're hearing in their setup, then make a quick little wager on the direction. If your tone stays light, it reads as curiosity, not interruption. A soft guess creates momentum without hijacking the story they're trying to tell. Picture your friend describing a "quick" meeting that somehow involved three managers and an unexplained calendar invite titled Alignment. Right when they hit the pause, you slide in with something like, "This feels like it went off the rails," then you shut up. That last part matters. The prediction is the spark, not the speech.

They'll either laugh and confirm, or correct you with even more detail, which is exactly what you want.

Tip 119: Use Predictions to Keep It Alive

A story gets better the moment it stops being a monologue. Predictions make it interactive because they give the teller a partner instead of an audience. They're also great for people who worry they're boring you. When you guess, you're showing them you're following the plot, not checking the exits. Here's an easy way to time it: wait for the "hinge" phrase. The moment they say "so then..." or "and that's when..." or they do that little inhale before the reveal, you give one playful forecast and let them take the wheel again.

If they confirm, you can stay with it by asking for one detail that puts you in the room: "What did you say right after that?" If they correct you, even better: "Okay, now I need the real version." Use it once per story, max. Too many predictions and you turn their moment into a guessing game show. One well-timed guess, though, makes the whole thing feel like you're in it together, which is the real point.

Chapter 54: Preview the Disagreement

Disagreeing without wrecking the vibe is a bit of an art. A lot of people avoid it entirely, smile and nod, then complain to someone else later. Others go straight from "I have a thought" to "verbal chainsaw," and wonder why people tense up around them. The problem usually isn't the opinion. It's the surprise. Relationship researcher John Gottman has spent decades studying how couples fight, stay together, or fall apart. One thing his work makes very clear: people handle disagreement way better when they know it's coming. When you suddenly drop "That's just wrong" into the middle of a sentence, their body goes into defense mode before their brain even catches up.

But if you preface it with something like, "I see it a bit differently on one point," you give their nervous system a tiny bit of warning. Enough time to think, "Okay, we're still okay, we just don't fully agree." That's the disagreement preview. It's one short line that separates them from their idea and slows everything down half a beat. "I'm mostly with you, but there's one part I see differently." "I love where you're going, I just want to push on one piece." You're saying, "You and I are still on the same team. I just want to argue with this specific thought."

That sounds small, but that little distinction is exactly what protects rapport while you stay honest.

Tip 120: Put a Soft Label on the Difference

Hard contradiction can sound like rejection, even when your point is valid. A soft label helps you disagree without detonating the tone.

Open with scope and shared ground: "I'm with you on most of that, and I see one part differently." Or, "I think we're close; the part I'd challenge is this." Those frames keep the relationship intact while still making your position clear.

Then deliver the difference plainly. No eye roll, no "actually," no superiority perfume. You are adding information, not grading their intelligence. That subtle framing keeps people listening instead of defending.

When you feel yourself about to say, "No, that's wrong," replace the shove with a label, then make your case. You'll notice fewer pointless escalations and better-quality disagreement, which is the kind that leaves both people smarter instead of just louder. That's usually where trust grows, not where it breaks.

Tip 121: Separate the Person from the Idea

Disagreement gets messy when it sounds like a verdict on the person instead of the idea. You can lower that risk with one sentence that separates the two.

Try: "I respect you, and I see this part differently." Or: "I get where you're coming from; I disagree with this specific piece." You are not softening your position. You're protecting the relationship while you hold it.

People often can handle disagreement. What they can't handle is feeling personally dismissed. Make the distinction explicit before you get into your reasoning.

Do this early, not after things have already gone sharp. It keeps the conversation in problem-solving mode and reduces the urge to defend identity. That single framing line can save a lot of cleanup later.

Chapter 55: Use Kind Speculation

There's a special kind of compliment that hits deeper than "Nice job." It's when someone looks at you, hears a bit of your story, then says, "I bet you handled that with so much patience," or "I'm guessing you were the calm one in that chaos." Not only they're praising the outcome, they're also guessing at the kind of person you were in that moment. That feels different. Studies on social attunement and "being known" keep landing on the same point: people love feeling positively "read." When someone makes a warm, reasonable guess about your intentions or character, it feels like they've been paying attention to your inner world, not just your behavior. It's flattering, but in a grounded way.

A kind speculation says, "This is how I see you," and if that picture is generous and believable, most people lean toward it. They even try to live up to it. That's the kind speculation move. Instead of just reacting to what happened, you add a light, positive guess about how they showed up. "I bet you were more prepared than everyone else." "I'm guessing you were probably the one keeping people calm." Done gently, it doesn't feel fake. It feels like someone is holding up a version of you that you actually like. And people tend to stick close to the ones who see them that way.

Tip 122: Make Kind Guesses About Their Best Self

Kind speculation only works if it's plausible. Telling someone who just admitted they panicked, "I bet you were completely calm the whole time," is going to feel off. Noticing the strength inside the mess lands much better. Something like, "I get the sense you still kept things moving, even while you were freaking out," is closer to the truth and still kind. Use this when they're telling a story that clearly cost them something: effort, courage, patience, care. Instead of stopping at, "Wow, that's a lot," add one small positive guess about how they probably showed up. You're giving language to a strength they might not name for themselves. Keep the tone light and observational, not intense or dramatic.

No sainthood speeches, just a simple, "Here's how I imagine you showed up," that leans toward their better side without overdoing it. Try it once with someone you know reasonably well: listen to a small story, then add one kind, realistic guess about how they probably handled it. Most of the time you'll get a shy smile or a quiet, "Yeah, I tried." That's your sign it landed.

Tip 123: Make a Kind Read

The sneaky power of this move is that it doesn't just describe reality, it gently shapes it. When you say, "I know you're probably being really considerate about how you worded that," they're more likely to stay considerate. When you tell someone, "You seem like the type who checks in on people," you're planting a seed they'll often water later.

You could use that deliberately to lift the tone of the interaction: Before a tough conversation: "I know you'll be honest and kind about this." When they're unsure: "I have a feeling you'll think about this carefully before you decide." After they share a dilemma: "You strike me as someone who'll handle that with a lot of empathy." You're not manipulating them. It's simply giving language to the version of them you already see. Most people are desperate for that kind of reflection, because their inner critic is usually running the opposite script.

When you're with someone who seems a bit unsure or hard on themselves, offer one kind, believable line about how they're likely to handle things at their best, then leave it alone. No repeating it, no sales pitch, no follow-up monologue. Just let them sit with how they live in your mind. A lot of the time they'll quietly lean toward that picture, and they won't forget who painted it for them.

Chapter 56: Echo a Shared Value

There are moments in conversation where you feel a quiet click that has nothing to do with hobbies, jobs, or favorite shows. It happens when someone says, "I just want it to be fair," or "What matters to me is being honest with people," and something in you goes, "Yep. That. That's my language." You're not bonding over coffee preferences anymore. You're bonding over how you think the world should work. That runs deeper. Psychologist Shalom Schwartz spent years mapping human values across different cultures. He kept finding the same thing: people are wildly different on the surface, but most of us organize our lives around a small set of core values like fairness, kindness, security, creativity, loyalty, or freedom.

When two people recognize that they share one of those, connection ramps up quickly. It stops feeling like two strangers comparing facts and starts feeling like two people standing on the same piece of ground. The shared value echo is about catching those moments on purpose. Someone uses a word like "fair," "kind," "respectful," "honest," "clear," and instead of letting it slide by, you mirror it back and link yourself to it. "Fairness matters to me too." "I care a lot about clarity as well." Short, simple, not dramatic. But that small echo tells them, "You and I are playing by a similar rulebook."

Trust builds faster when it's tied to something meaningful, not just "We both like the same TV show."

Tip 124: Listen for Value Words

People leak their values in the words they repeat. "I just want it to feel fair." "I hate when people aren't honest." "I really appreciate straightforwardness." Those are not just adjectives. They are flags, and your job is to notice them and gently pick one up.

Instead of jumping straight to your opinion, pause and echo the value. "Fairness matters to me too." "I care a lot about honesty as well." "Respect is a big thing for me too, so I get why that bothered you." You're validating what they care about while quietly saying, "I'm built a little like you." That shifts the tone from "me vs. you" to "us vs. the problem."

In your next real conversation, listen for just one value word. When you hear it, stop yourself from rushing past it. Echo it, link yourself to it with a short "me too" sentence, then continue. You'll usually see their body language open up, because you just confirmed that you get them at a deeper level than "I heard the story."

Tip 125: Use Shared Values in Tough Moments

Shared values are useful in hard conversations because they give both people something stable to stand on. Not agreement on tactics - agreement on what matters.

Before you argue details, name the value: "I think we both care about being fair here." "We both want this done well, not just fast." "I know we both care about trust in this relationship."

That doesn't erase conflict, but it changes its shape. You're no longer two opponents proving each other wrong. You're two people trying to protect the same principle with different strategies.

If things start escalating, return to the value line and ask, "Given that, what option gets us closest?" It keeps the conversation from collapsing into point-scoring and helps both sides stay oriented to the bigger purpose.

Chapter 57: Lead with We

Nothing makes advice land worse than that subtle scolding vibe. "What you should do is…" and instantly your brain pulls the emergency brake. You feel judged, cornered, or like you're in some surprise coaching session you didn't sign up for. The content might be helpful, but the grammar is rude. Social psychologists like Susan Fiske and her colleagues have looked at how inclusive language changes the way people feel about each other. One big finding: "we" phrasing feels more cooperative and less threatening than "you" phrasing. "You need to be more clear" sounds like a verdict. "How could we make this clearer?" sounds like partnership. Same basic direction, totally different emotional cost. That's the "we-frame" suggestion.

Instead of standing outside their life pointing at it, you verbally step inside the moment with them. "How can we approach this?" "What could we try here?" "How do we want to handle this?" You're not pretending to carry all their problems, you're just signaling, "I'm on your side, not above you." If you speak like a team, people start to feel like one.

Tip 126: Swap "You Should" for "How Could We…"

A lot of advice starts with, "Here's what you need to do." Honest, maybe, but it puts the other person on the defensive before they've even heard the idea. A small language swap makes that same advice feel like collaboration instead of a performance review.

A simple move is to reframe suggestions like this: Instead of: "You should talk to your boss about that." Try: "How could we imagine you bringing that up with your boss?" Instead of: "You need to set better boundaries." Try: "How could we set some boundaries there so it feels better for you?" Instead of: "You've got to be clearer in your messages." Try: "How could we make your messages clearer without adding more work?" Instead of taking the problem out of their hands, you're just choosing to stand next to them while you look at it together. That small adjustment makes most people more open, because the suggestion feels co-created rather than dropped on them from above.

When you next feel a "You should…" lining up, treat it as a little cue. Take a breath, swap it for a "we" plus a question, and watch how it lands. The idea stays the same, but it shows up as partnership instead of instructions.

Tip 127: Use "We" to Lower Shame

People don't just resist advice because they're stubborn. They resist it because advice often carries a side order of shame. "You messed up. Here's how to stop messing up." The we-frame drains a lot of that sting. It says, "You're not broken, you're human, and this is the kind of thing we figure out together." You could use "we" to normalize and move things forward: "We've all put things off like that. How do we want to tackle this one?" "We can probably find a simpler way to handle that next time." "We'll figure out a version of this that feels more like you." You don't have to pretend you see everything the same way.

The real move is not leaving them alone in the role of "problem person." When the issue sits between you instead of inside them, it's a lot easier for them to stay in the conversation instead of shutting down or going

194

straight into defense. In one slightly sensitive moment this week, when you're about to offer a correction, a suggestion, or a different perspective, wrap it in "we" once. "We can tweak this." "We'll sort it out." Watch how quickly their shoulders loosen. If you consistently talk like you're on their side, they'll start to feel like you are, and that's when real change and real closeness both get a lot easier.

Chapter 58: Before and After Question

Some stories sound flat even when the content is big. "I changed careers, it was great." "We used to argue a lot, but now we're fine." Cool, but that could be the caption on a stock photo. What actually makes a story land is contrast. Before and after. Old world, new world. How it was, how it is now. That is where the meaning lives. Narrative researchers have found that people experience their lives as stories with turning points. When you highlight the "before" and the "after," the brain locks in on the transformation. It feels more real, more important, and more satisfying. Asking someone, "What was it like before that happened?" is a tiny move with a big effect.

It nudges their memory to pull up not just the outcome, but the journey. You're helping them tell a richer story about their own life. A simple way to do this is to tug gently on the contrast whenever someone mentions a change, an improvement, a disaster, or a big decision. "What was it like before you made that shift?" "How were things different for you back then?" The question pulls more detail, more emotion, and more self-awareness out of them. You're no longer just hearing the headline. You're walking through the chapters around it. Otherwise the story reads like a movie trailer where someone forgot to include the movie.

Tip 128: Ask for the Before

When someone says, "After that, things were so much better," it's tempting to nod and move on. But the part that makes the story powerful is usually sitting just off-screen in the "before." If you don't visit that earlier version, their big turning point lands like a slogan instead of a shift. A simple move is to pause on their transition word—after that, since then, from that point—and tilt the conversation backward: "Hold on, what was it like before you made that change?" or "What did a normal week look like for you back then?" Ask once, then get out of the way.

Let them walk you into the old world: the routines, the stress, the numbness, the version of themselves they almost forgot they were living with. As they talk, they often hear their own contrast more clearly: I was exhausted all the time, I didn't realize how much I was putting up with, I was just on autopilot. Now, when they come back to the "after," both of you can actually feel the shift instead of just labeling it.

Tip 129: Use Contrast to Find the Turning Point

When you want people to feel progress, show contrast. Not hype, not big claims - contrast. Before and after. Then and now.

"Before, every check-in ended with confusion. Now we leave with one clear next step." "Before, I avoided this conversation. Now I can actually stay in it without spiraling."

Contrast makes change visible. Without it, even real growth feels vague and easy to dismiss.

When you're describing a shift, use one concrete example from each side of the line. Keep it simple and specific. People trust progress more when they can picture it. And once they can picture it, they're more likely to repeat it.

Section: Continuity & Endings

Repair gets you back to neutral. Continuity is how you move beyond neutral into momentum. This section focuses on staying connected after the conversation is over.

What happens after a conversation matters as much as what happened inside it.

These chapters focus on closure, follow-through, and continuity signals: how to end cleanly, preserve momentum, and make future contact feel natural.

If interactions fade despite good moments, this section will help you convert one-off conversations into ongoing relationships.

Chapter 59: Build Running References

Some of the best relationships are basically a long string of "this is just like that time when..." moments. Two people see something out in the wild, glance at each other, and you can tell they're mentally dragging it into a private folder called "ours." A ridiculous meeting. A strange coffee shop regular. A type of email everyone hates. Once it's in the folder, it becomes shorthand. "Oh no, it's that guy again," and the other person instantly gets it. Psycholinguist Herbert Clark studied how people build "common ground" in conversations. One of his big conclusions was that shared references, especially external ones, make cooperation smoother and connection stronger.

When two people can point at the same thing and say, "That, right there," they stop needing paragraphs of explanation. A quick callback like, "This is a good example of that thing we were talking about earlier," isn't just commentary. It's cement. You're turning a random moment into a joint mental bookmark. Mutual reference building is what grows that private folder over time. You grab something outside of both of you, then link it to a previous conversation, idea, or joke. "This feels like that project we survived last year." "This guy is exactly like the 'I'll circle back' person we talked about." It does a few things at once.

It proves you remember past moments, it shows you're actively mapping the world together, and it creates that easy "we see things the same way" feeling that makes people relax around you.

Tip 130: Turn Moments Into "This Is Just Like…"

Any time you spot a situation that fits something you and the other person have already talked about, you've got a chance to add another inside reference. It can be serious or completely dumb. The charm is in saying the connection out loud. So you're in a meeting and it's pure chaos, and you lean over and say, "This is exactly that kind of circus we were laughing about last week." Or you get a terrible corporate email and go, "Okay, this is that 'email nightmare' you told me about in real life." Small, throwaway lines, but they do a lot of quiet work.

They say: I remember what you said, I'm paying attention now, and I'm looking at this through a shared lens, not just my own. Even when the topic is silly, it adds a tiny "we" to the moment. Pick one person and one theme you already have going—an annoying behavior, a type of client, a running joke, a shared hobby. When you see a live example, tag it with a quick "This is just like that thing we talked about." One sentence, then move on. You've just turned a random moment into another brick in the little private world between you.

Tip 131: Use Callbacks to Say "I Remember You"

Mutual references really shine over time. When you call back to something from an earlier conversation, you're doing more than being clever. You're sending a quiet message: "I didn't just nod back then. I kept it." That alone builds a lot of warmth. One practical route is to do this with anything that stuck out before: A phrase they used: "This is another one of your 'beautiful mess' situations." A value they named:

"This is hitting your fairness radar again, isn't it?" A story they told: "This reminds me of that first job you described where no one knew what they were doing." You're building a shared mental model, piece by piece.

They start to feel like you're not just hearing their stories, you're actually integrating them. That makes you feel less like a passing character and more like someone who's genuinely in their corner. If you'd like something simple to play with, think of one memorable thing someone told you recently. When you're with them, wait for a moment that vaguely echoes it, then drop a light callback: "This is giving me flashbacks to your story about…" Watch for the reaction. Even a small smile or "Oh my God, yes" means you landed it. You just added one more private reference to the shared map between you, and those maps are where closeness quietly lives.

Chapter 60: Shrink the Timeline

You know that feeling when you ask, "So what happened?" and suddenly you're getting the prequel, the origin story, the spin-off, and the director's cut. They start in 2014, you were asking about a thing from Tuesday, and now no one remembers the original question. They're not doing anything wrong. Their brain just doesn't know how far back you want them to go. Conversation analysts inspired by Harvey Sacks noticed this exact problem. When people are unsure where to begin, they either overshare and wander, or freeze and give you almost nothing. But when you quietly set a "context radius," like "Can you walk me through just the last week of this?"

or "Can we start from when you joined the team?", something shifts. The story tightens. They feel less pressure to tell you everything and more freedom to tell you something useful. The context radius move is simply deciding out loud how much backstory you are asking for. "Give me the short version from yesterday." "Can we start from when this became a real problem?" "Walk me through just the last part, from when they emailed you." It gives structure, and humans love structure more than we admit. Now they're doing a clear, bounded task instead of performing their entire life on stage. That makes sharing feel safer, lighter, and a lot less tiring for both of you.

Tip 132: Tighten the Time Window

When people don't know where to start, they usually go way too far back. That's not about drama. It's anxiety. "If I don't give enough context, they might misunderstand." You can calm that fear by shrinking the timeline for them. You're basically saying, "You don't have to build me the whole house, just show me this one room." You can set the radius with tiny, clear prompts: "Can you walk me through just what happened this morning?" "Can we start from when the new manager came in?" "Talk me through the last meeting where this came up." Notice how each one quietly tells them what to skip. Childhood. Old jobs. Entire relationship histories. Off the table.

They get to zoom in. That kind of focus feels like relief, not restriction. In your next conversation with someone who tends to ramble or feel overwhelmed, give them a time frame before they dive in. "Can you give me the last week version?" Then stay inside that frame with your follow up questions. You'll probably walk away with a clearer story, and they will walk away feeling oddly proud of how well they explained it.

Tip 133: Use Radius Cues for Safety

People open up faster when they know how far they have to go. If the emotional distance is unclear, many will play it safe and stay vague.

You can lower that uncertainty with a radius cue: "Give me the short version." "Only what you're comfortable sharing." "If you're up for it, we can go deeper."

Those lines do one important thing: they put choice back in their hands. Choice reduces pressure. Reduced pressure increases honesty.

Use this when a topic feels sensitive or loaded. You don't need to extract a perfect answer. You're creating a conversation where they can choose the depth without feeling trapped. That alone makes most people more willing to speak plainly.

Run this as a baseline behavior. With practice, the cumulative effect is bigger than any single moment.

Chapter 61: Hand Them the Spotlight

You know that little spark people get when the conversation hits their niche? Someone mentions wine, running form, niche sci-fi, or organizational systems, and suddenly one person in the group sits up a little straighter. That's their territory. A lot of us accidentally trample that moment by jumping in with our own half-baked take instead of handing them the spotlight they were built for. Social psychologists Susan Fiske and Steven Neuberg have written about how we tend to like people who recognize and use our strengths. When someone treats you as the "go-to" person on a topic, you do not just feel smart. You feel valued. Like your weird pocket of knowledge has a home.

A simple line like, "You'd explain this better than I could," or "You're the expert here," is not just flattery. It tells the other person, "I see what you're good at, and I want everyone else to see it too." That's the "Let Them Shine" hand-off. A topic pops up, you know they have something good in the vault, so instead of claiming the floor, you give it away on purpose. Think of it less as shrinking and more as curating the moment. People remember the person who made space for them to be impressive far more than the one who tried to hog the mic.

Tip 134: Point the Spotlight, Then Step Back

When you hear a topic enter the chat that lines up perfectly with their skills or experience, treat it like a chance to redirect the spotlight. You're basically acting as a friendly MC. One clean sentence is all it takes. You can say something along the lines of, "Honestly, you'd explain this better than I could," or, "You know this stuff way more than I do, what's your take?" In a more playful setting, it might be, "This is literally your zone, do you want to take this one?" Different flavors, same move: you're flagging their expertise and inviting them in. Then, the important part: actually shut up.

Turn your body slightly toward them, keep your eyes on them, and let them talk without swooping back in after four seconds. You just gave them a little stage. Let them stand on it. Pick one person in your life who clearly has a "thing" they're good at. When that topic shows up, run a deliberate hand-off. Name their strength, give them the floor, and then stay in listening mode. You'll often see them light up, and they'll quietly log away, "They notice what I'm good at, and they're not threatened by it."

Tip 135: Use Hand-Offs to Warm the Group

This move is lethal (in a good way) in group settings. Meetings, group chats, dinners. Instead of letting the loudest person dominate, you can tilt the room toward people who'd never grab the floor for themselves but have killer things to say. That makes you come across as confident and generous at the same time. In a group, try lines like: "You've actually done this before, right? I'd love to hear your take." "You had a really good point about this the other day, want to share it?" "You're the one with real experience here, how do you see it?" You're doing three jobs at once.

You're boosting them, you're improving the quality of the conversation by bringing in actual expertise, and you're signaling to everyone else, "This is a room where other people get to shine." That kind of energy is rare, which is exactly why it's attractive. If you want a simple practice, in your next group setting, commit to at least one intentional hand-off. Scan for the quiet person with the relevant strength, name it out loud, and invite them in. With practice, people will start to associate you with that specific feeling: "When they're around, I feel more seen, more capable, and more included." You can't buy that kind of reputation. You build it one spotlight at a time.

Chapter 62: Ask What Changed

Every so often, someone says something about their life that sounds oddly permanent. "I've always been bad with conflict." "Things are just like this with my family." "I'm not a confident person." Your brain hears it and knows that is probably not the whole story. Nobody is one static thing forever. But most people talk like their current state has always been true, because it feels simpler than sorting through how it actually changed. Narrative researcher Dan McAdams has spent decades studying how people turn their life into a story. One of his big insights is that meaning lives in contrast. Before and after. Then and now. "I used to be like this, now I'm more like that."

When you ask a simple question like, "Was it always like that, or did it shift over time?", you flip on the light in that part of their story. Instead of repeating a label, they start remembering a process. Evolution. They're not just "bad at conflict" anymore. They're someone who went from one pattern to another, even if they never noticed it until you asked. With the contrast curiosity cue, you're not grilling them. You're simply inviting them to look at how something became the way it is, instead of treating it as random. Most people enjoy that more than they expect.

It is oddly satisfying to notice, "Oh, I've actually changed," or, "Huh, this really did get worse after that specific thing." You end up as the person who does not just collect headlines, but helps them see the storyline running underneath.

Tip 136: Ask: Has It Always Been Like This?

When someone drops a big general statement, your temptation might be to argue with it or reassure them. "I'm terrible at friendships." "No you're not, you're great!" Nice sentiment, zero depth. The contrast curiosity cue takes a different route. You zoom out in time instead of fighting the label. Try saying: "Has it always felt that way, or did it change at some point?" "Was it like this even when you were younger, or is this more recent?" "Do you feel like it's been the same over the years, or has it shifted?" One question, then you shut up and let them look around in their own memory.

Very often they'll say something like, "Actually, I used to be more outgoing," or "Honestly, it got way worse after that job," or "Come to think of it, I've gotten better at this, just not where I want to be." You didn't tell them who they are. You helped them notice that their story is already moving. That alone can feel hopeful, even if nothing is "fixed" yet. You become the person who helps them spot motion where they thought everything was stuck.

Tip 137: Hunt the Shift, Not the Diagnosis

When something feels off, most people go hunting for a diagnosis too early. "What's wrong with this person?" "What's the core issue?" That's usually too abstract, too soon.

Start with the shift instead. Ask: "When did this start feeling different?" "What changed right before that?" Shifts are observable. Diagnoses are guesses.

Once you find the shift, the next step usually becomes obvious: a boundary changed, a deadline moved, a trust moment got missed, a new pressure entered the system. Now you're working with evidence, not projection.

This approach keeps conversations grounded and less personal. You are mapping what changed, not assigning blame. That makes it easier for both people to stay engaged long enough to actually fix something.

If the move feels new, that's fine. Prioritize presence over polish and fluency will catch up.

Chapter 63: Follow the Micro-Shift

You can tell more about a person from the half-second changes in their voice than from the actual words sometimes. They're talking at one level, then suddenly their tone softens, their eyes drop for a moment, or a tiny smile sneaks in and disappears. Most people steamroll right over that and keep the conversation on the surface. The moment passes, and so does the chance to actually connect. Psychologist Tania Singer's work on emotional attunement suggests that people feel deeply safe and bonded when someone notices their inner shifts, not just their outer story. You don't need to read minds. You just have to catch those little changes and gently say, "I saw that. Do you want to say more?"

A simple line like, "Your tone changed a bit when you said that, what made that part feel different?" can turn a regular chat into something that actually matters. Think of this as an emotional micro-shift invite: a tiny gesture where you name what you noticed and offer them the option to stay with it. No diagnosis, no pushing, just a quiet "if you want to go there, I am here." For a lot of people, that level of attention lands like water in a dry place and makes the conversation feel less like talking into the air and more like being met.

Tip 138: Name the Shift, Then Leave Space

The trick is to keep it light and observational, not dramatic or accusatory. You're not saying, "You seem deeply wounded," you're saying, "Something in you just moved a bit, and I'm curious." Small and soft wins here. It can sound like, "Your voice went a bit quieter when you mentioned your brother. What changed there?" or, "You suddenly lit up when you talked about that trip, what made that part so good?" Short, concrete, and tied to something you actually saw or heard. Once you have named it, stop talking. Hold eye contact, keep your posture open, and let a little silence hang. That pause is where they decide whether to brush it off or go deeper.

If they steer away, you respect that and move on. If they say, "Yeah, that part is actually hard," or "Honestly, that was the best part of my year," you've just crossed into real territory. As a practice, pick one conversation where you're already listening closely. Notice one small change in tone, pace, or expression, reflect it in a single sentence with a soft question, and then stay still. Many people will take that as the permission they didn't know they were waiting for.

Tip 139: Follow Their Shift, Not Your Agenda

Most of us steer conversations based on what we find interesting. Micro-shift invites flip that. You're letting their nervous system tell you what matters, then building the conversation around that instead of your favorite theme. That is unbelievably validating. Here's how that might look in real life: They're giving you a pretty neutral rundown of work, then their tone softens for half a second when they mention one coworker. Rather than asking about the whole workplace again, you zoom in: "You sounded different when you mentioned Alex just now. What's the story there?" Or they're talking about a stressful week, all in the same flat tone, then suddenly laugh a little at one tiny part.

You catch it: "That bit made you laugh. What was funny about that moment?" You're letting their micro-reactions draw the map. It tells them, "I'm not just listening to the plot. I'm listening to you in the plot."

If you want a simple rep, spend one conversation in "emotion radar" mode. Don't force depth. Just notice one small change in tone, pace, or expression and follow that instead of your default agenda. That one choice often turns a decent chat into a real one.

Tip 140: Flag One Next Step

You can use forward anchors right in the middle of a topic. Think of them as conversational bookmarks that also double as fuel. They tell the other person, "I'm here with you now, and I'm already invested in what comes after this too." That feels surprisingly good. Simple ways to do it: "Finish this story, then I want to hear how your presentation went." "I want to come back to your trip later, but first, tell me what happened with your manager." "After this, I'm curious how you've been feeling about being back in the office." You're stacking the deck in favor of momentum. Even if this thread ends naturally, you've already agreed on what to pick up next.

That takes the pressure off both of you to magically conjure a new topic in the moment. In your next catch up, pick one thing you know you want to hear about, and name it as a "later": "At some point I want the full story on that move, but how are you feeling today?" People usually relax, because they can tell you're not just killing time. You're mentally in it for more than one question at a time. There's a fine line between creating momentum and making someone feel like they are in a structured interview.

Chapter 64: Say You Don't Know

There's a special kind of social panic that hits when someone brings up a topic you barely understand. Crypto regulation. Niche literature. Some new framework everyone at work pretends they have read. A lot of people respond by faking it. They throw out vague phrases, nod hard, and pray no one asks a follow up. It feels safer in the moment, but it quietly kills connection. You cannot relax if you're busy hiding. Research on intellectual humility by psychologist Elizabeth Krumrei-Mancuso suggests something counterintuitive. People often respond better when you can say, "I don't really know much about that." The key is what comes next. If you follow it with, "What's your take?"

or "Can you walk me through how you see it?", the "confession" stops being a weakness and becomes an invitation. You're telling them, "I'm not here to impress you. I'm here to learn from you." That is incredibly disarming. This is the shared curiosity confession. Instead of pretending you are in the know, you name your ignorance out loud and turn it into a bridge. You lower your own status a notch on purpose, then raise theirs by asking for their view. Done well, it feels honest, playful, and strangely confident. You're basically saying, "I'm secure enough to not know everything." That vibe is a lot more charming than the human Wikipedia act most of us try to run.

Tip 141: Turn "I Don't Know" Into Curiosity

People often panic when they don't know something and try to hide it with confident nodding. You can feel the strain immediately, because now you're doing theater instead of conversation. A cleaner move is to say the obvious thing out loud and pivot straight into curiosity.

A useful shape is: "I actually don't know much about that. How do you see it?" Or, "I've heard of it, but I'm fuzzy on it. What matters most about it to you?" That second sentence is the whole trick. You're not asking for a lecture. You're asking for their version, which is usually where the interesting part lives anyway.

Test this once today on a topic where you'd normally fake it. Keep the tone light, ask one follow-up, and then listen without jumping in to prove you're smart. Most people visibly relax when nobody is pretending. The conversation gets better because the performance ends and real exchange begins.

Tip 142: Use Not-Knowing to Equalize

Admitting ignorance is especially powerful when you're the one with more status or confidence in the room. Leader, older sibling, "social one" in the group, doesn't matter. When you say, "I don't know, what do you think?" you level the ground and make it safer for other people to contribute.

Use it on purpose. In a group: "I'm not sure about the best route here, anyone have a take?" One-on-one: "I don't have a clean answer yet. How are you thinking about it?" In disagreement: "I might be missing something. What am I not seeing from your side?" Underneath, you're signaling three things: I'm not pretending to be all-knowing. Your perspective is welcome. We can figure this out together.

Try it once where you'd normally default to giving the answer. Trade certainty for shared curiosity and notice how quickly people lean in.

Tip 143: Plant Curiosity Seeds

A heavy, soul-baring question isn't required to move a conversation below surface level. A small "I've been wondering..." line can act like a side door. It keeps things casual, but points the energy somewhere more interesting than traffic, deadlines, or who's streaming what. Instead of launching straight into, "So what's your biggest fear?", you drop something like, "I've always wondered how people can tell when they're in the right kind of relationship for them," or, "Lately I've been thinking about what actually makes a place feel like home." It is not a demand.

It is just a thought placed between you with an implied, "We can stay here for a minute if you're into it." If they lean in, you can nudge it open with a simple, "How do you see it?" or "Where do you land on that?" If they answer lightly or change the subject, you roll with it. The question still did its job: it shifted the mood from pure logistics to something a little more reflective. Use it with someone you already enjoy talking to. Once the basic catch-up is out of the way, drop one real curiosity you have had lately. Keep it honest and unfancy.

Chapter 65: Repair Small Friction Quickly

Small social friction adds up fast. A delayed reply. A dropped thread. A tangent that eats the point. A compliment that gets awkward. A tense moment where your body language does too much. None of these are disasters by themselves, but together they can make conversations feel heavier than they need to.

This chapter is about quick repair moves that keep connection intact without overexplaining. You acknowledge the miss, reset the lane, and keep going with warmth. Most people don't need perfection from you. They just need clear signals that you're still present, still respectful, and still in the conversation.

Tip 144: Patch the Gap, Not Your Character

The aim is not an essay about your calendar. It's one clean line that does three things: Acknowledge the delay, Humanize it, Reaffirm that you care about the person or the topic. That can sound like: "Sorry for the slow reply, this week got away from me, but I really liked what you said here." "Late response on my part, I wanted to answer properly when my brain came back online." "I know this is a delayed response, but I didn't want to skip over your message." Then you answer like a normal person. No ten-paragraph apology, no self-dragging monologue about how terrible you are at texting. Over-apologizing shifts the focus from them to your guilt.

A simple acknowledgement plus warmth gets the job done. You can use the same move with older threads too: "This is a very 'replying way later' message, but I've been thinking about what you said about your job." "Late circle back, but I wanted to ask how that presentation ended up going." You're telling them: the conversation didn't die, it just stalled on your side and you're restarting the engine. One sentence, then back into connection.

Tip 145: Name the Lag Out Loud

Real-life lag happens all the time. You disappear for a while, you dodge a topic, you go quiet at the worst moment, then you act normal and hope nobody noticed. They noticed. The awkwardness usually comes from pretending the gap never happened.

Use one sentence to clear it: "I know I've been off the grid, I'm glad we're talking now." Or, "I never answered what you asked me last time, can we go back to it?" Even mid-conversation, "I went quiet for a second because I wanted to say this right," works. Short, honest, then continue. Don't turn it into a courtroom statement.

The pattern is simple: name the lag, give a human-sized reason, re-enter with warmth. Think of it as wiping fog off the windshield, not confessing your sins. One clean acknowledgment plus one real follow-up question is usually enough to drop the tension and get you both back into an actual conversation.

Tip 146: Respect the Tangent, Then Return

The social miss here usually shows up in two forms. One is letting the tangent completely eat the original topic. The other is slamming on the brakes with "Anyway, back to what I was saying," which can feel abrupt. A good side-track return sits in the middle. You acknowledge the detour, keep the good vibe, and bring the first thread back into the room.

Keep it light: "That was a great detour, can we circle back to what you were saying about your manager?" or "We zoomed off for a second, but I still want to hear how you were feeling before the move." You're not scolding anyone for drifting. You're showing you remember what mattered.

Tip 147: Let the Compliment Land

Many people treat compliments like hot food: receive, panic, deflect. "It was nothing." "I got lucky." "Team effort." You think you're being humble, but often it sounds like you're refusing the gift.

Try a cleaner move: "Thank you, I appreciate that." Full stop. If you need one extra line, keep it short: "I worked hard on that one." That's enough confidence to receive praise without turning it into theater.

This isn't ego training. It's social ease training. When you accept a compliment directly, the other person feels their kindness landed where intended. No awkward cleanup, no forced argument about whether you're secretly bad.

Run a one-day experiment: every compliment gets a simple thank-you and no deflection. You'll feel odd for a few rounds, then normal. People around you will feel the difference almost immediately. You will too, because your nervous system stops bracing for praise like it's a trap.

Tip 148: Use Gentle Gestures to Calm the Room

Gestures can either make you feel warm and clear, or intense and overwhelming. The trick is in the speed and size. Fast, sharp movements can feel like you're jabbing your point at someone. Slow, open ones feel like you're laying it out on the table for both of you to look at. Think in terms of soft, guiding movements.

An open palm facing slightly upward when you ask, "How does that land for you?" A small smoothing motion downward when you say, "Let's slow this down for a second." A relaxed circling motion when you're tying things together: "So all of this connects to…" These little cues tell the other person, without words, "This is shared space, not an attack." That matters a lot when you're giving feedback, explaining something complex, or talking about something that could make them tense. For one conversation where you know you'll be explaining something, give yourself a quiet rule: slow, open gestures only. Palms visible, movements smooth, no stabbing finger points, no flailing.

Let your hands trace the structure of what you're saying instead of acting out your anxiety. You'll probably notice two things: you feel more grounded and less rushed, and they look more relaxed and tuned in. Your body is doing some of the emotional smoothing so your words don't have to carry the whole load.

Chapter 66: Offer a Tiny Choice

Nothing kills vibe faster than feeling like a passenger in your own conversation. Someone launches into a twenty-minute story you didn't ask for, picks the topic, pace, and depth, then proudly announces, "Anyway, that's me." You were technically there, but you were not in it. You were just the audience. Psychologists Edward Deci and Richard Ryan, the self-determination guys, have repeatedly found that humans are highly sensitive to autonomy. Even tiny choices, like picking a pen color or choosing a snack, make us feel more invested and connected. The same thing applies to conversations. When you offer small decisions like, "Want the short version or the full story?"

or "Should we start with work or life?", you're not being overly polite. You're quietly telling the other person, "You're part of steering this, not just sitting through it." That's the shared decision micro-move. You hand them a small choice about the direction, length, or focus of what happens next. "Should we start here or there?" "Want to stay on this or switch topics?" "Do you want advice or just a listener?" The choice is tiny, but the effect is not. You're building a two-way street from the first few seconds, and people warm up fast when they feel like their preferences actually shape the conversation.

Tip 149: Offer Tiny Forks in the Road

Skip the big "What should this entire conversation be about?" moment. Micro-choices are enough. Offer two paths and let them steer the first turn: "Do you want the quick version or the full story?" or "Should we start with your week or mine?" Then follow what they pick. If they choose short, give the highlight reel, not a director's cut. If they choose your week first, go first and hand it back. The value isn't politeness. It's proving, in real time, that their preference changes what happens. Pick one person today and drop in a tiny fork like that early in the conversation. Let them decide which direction you take.

Watch how quickly their body language shifts from passive to engaged. Being asked, however simply, makes people lean in.

Tip 150: Give Agency While You Lead

Some of the best places to use shared decisions are moments where you'd normally plow ahead. You're the one telling the story, giving context, or offering help, so your instinct is to take full control. Instead, slip in one small choice before you continue: "I've got a couple of thoughts; do you want straight advice or just someone to react with you?" or "We can keep talking about this, or switch to something lighter. What are you up for?" You're still leading. You're just leaving one window cracked for their voice. That small bit of control often changes the emotional temperature fast: less trapped, less managed, more like they're in it with you.

In your next "serious" conversation, right before you take the floor, add one shared decision line. Let them pick the flavor of the next few minutes. It will not just make the conversation smoother. It will also quietly mark you as the kind of person who knows how to include people without making a big deal out of it. That is social gold.

Chapter 67: Tell Them Why You're Taking Notes

There's nothing quite like opening up to someone and watching them... pull out a notebook. Or start typing mid-sentence. Suddenly your brain goes from "I'm sharing something real" to "Am I being evaluated? Is this a performance review? Are they building a case file?" The words might still be flowing, but part of you just left the room. In work settings, coaching, or even deep friendships, note-taking can be a real act of care. You're trying to remember the good stuff, track ideas, or keep from losing the threads that matter. But if you don't explain what you're doing, it's very easy for the other person to read it as analysis, judgment, or distance.

Unexplained writing can make people feel like they're under a microscope instead of in a conversation. That's where the note-taking transparency move comes in. When you start jotting things down, you add one quick, human line like, "I'm just writing this so I don't lose the good parts," or, "I want to remember how you said that." Now the behavior has a clear story. The scribbling reads as care and attention, not silent evaluation. And most people secretly like knowing their words are worth capturing. It feels like proof that what they're saying isn't just evaporating into the air.

Tip 151: Name the Notebook Before They Wonder

The second you pull out a notebook without context, people start guessing. Are you judging me? Are you writing down mistakes? Did this become a performance review and nobody told me? You can prevent all of that with one line before the pen hits the page.

Say something like, "I'm writing this down because that was a great point and I don't want to lose it," or, "Let me note that so I remember it exactly." Then keep listening like a person, not like a court reporter: look up, nod, respond in real time. The aim is to make your note-taking feel like attention, not distance.

Use this in your next one-on-one where you know you'll capture details. Pick your sentence in advance so you don't improvise awkwardly in the moment. The shift is immediate. Once they know the notebook is there to hold value, not pass judgment, they relax and keep talking with more openness.

Tip 152: Let Notes Catch Wins, Not Just Problems

If the only time you write things down is when something's wrong, people will eventually associate your notebook with bad news. You can change that by capturing good moments too and occasionally saying so. When they say something sharp or do something well, you might pause with, "I want to keep that, it's a really clear way of seeing it," or, "That's a big win, I'm noting it so it doesn't get lost." Now the act of writing becomes a small compliment: this mattered enough to save. Try this with someone you regularly talk to about work, goals, or hard stuff.

The next time they have a win or offer a useful insight, write it down where they can see and give one short reason why. No speech or fanfare. With practice, they'll start to associate your note-taking with being valued, not evaluated, which makes them a lot more willing to keep opening up.

Chapter 68: Help Without Making It Weird

There's a kind of quiet charm that never makes it into self-help posts. It's not the big grand gesture or the "Look at me being helpful" moment. It's the tiny assist that barely gets noticed, but changes how the interaction feels. You slide a pen across the table before they even realize they need one. You pull up the right link while they're mid-sentence and drop it in the chat. You quietly remind them of the name they're searching for without making it a big deal. No spotlight, no speech. Just smooth. Researchers like Frank Flynn and Vanessa Lake have looked at how people respond to help that's subtle versus help that's loud. The surprising part?

People actually form stronger bonds with those who help in quiet, unobtrusive ways than with the ones who turn generosity into a performance. When your help doesn't steal the scene, the other person feels cared for, not indebted or exposed. It's the social equivalent of fixing a snag in someone's sweater without announcing it to the room. The "Invisible Help" cue is all about those micro-assists. You're not swooping in as the hero. You're just removing tiny bits of friction from the moment, almost as an afterthought. You refill their water while you're already up. You send the document everyone's trying to remember. You clarify a detail so they don't have to stumble.

Done right, it reads as "I'm with you" instead of "You needed me." That distinction matters a lot.

Tip 153: Help Quietly and Keep It Theirs

The easiest way to use invisible help is to look for tiny things that let them keep their flow. If they're telling a story and searching for a name, you offer it low-key. If they're presenting in a meeting and can't find the file, you drop it in the chat without commentary. You're greasing the gears, not taking over the machine. The key is to act like it's the most natural thing in the world. No play-by-play, no "Here, let me rescue this," no joking about how lost they'd be without you. You just smooth the path and let them stay in the foreground. From the outside, it looks like things are simply going well.

From the inside, they feel oddly supported and a little more relaxed, even if they can't quite say why. When you're in a group or one-on-one, look for a single small chance to make things easier without saying a word about it. Hand over what they're reaching for. Fix the tiny glitch. Supply the missing detail. Then let the conversation roll on like that was always how it was going to go.

Tip 154: Skip the Debt, Keep the Warmth

A lot of helpful behavior accidentally creates pressure. You jump in big, they feel like they owe you. That can make people pull back instead of closer. Invisible help sidesteps that. The aim isn't, "Now you must thank me forever." It's, "I had your back for a second, no strings attached." If they say, "Oh, thanks for grabbing that," a simple "Of course," "Anytime," or "Yeah, no problem," is enough. If they go bigger with, "You always save me in these meetings," you can smile and say something like, "We've all got each other," and steer the focus back to whatever they were saying. No

self-erasing "It was nothing," and no victory lap about
how they'd fall apart without you.

Handled this way, your help starts to feel like part
of the normal fabric of the relationship. They don't feel
pressured to even the score. They just get a steady,
background sense that when they're out there doing
their thing, you're somewhere nearby, quietly making
it easier to shine.

Chapter 69: Return Compliments with Grace

People often treat compliments like hot potatoes. Someone says, "You did great in that meeting," and the response is either a mumble, a deflection, or a panicked joke about how you nearly had a stroke. Compliment over, moment wasted. The social equivalent of hanging up mid-call. Psychologist Shelly Gable studies something called "capitalization," which is a fancy way of asking, "What happens when someone shares something positive with you?" Her research suggests that how we respond to good moments, praise, or wins has a strong impact on relationship quality. When you receive something positive and then build on it, the bond deepens.

When you shut it down, shrug it off, or make it awkward, the moment just dies on the table. That's where the compliment return path comes in. Instead of letting praise be a one-way spotlight that makes you squirm, you catch it, let it land, then gently send a bit of appreciation back. "Thank you, that means a lot. I really liked how you backed me up in there too." Or, "Thanks, and honestly, your feedback last week helped a ton." Now the moment isn't just "Look at me." It's "Look at what we did here." This works not just with compliments, but with any small positive moment someone shares. You're turning a loose spark into actual warmth between you.

Tip 155: Catch the Compliment, Share the Credit

This move has two beats, and both matter. Beat one: receive the compliment without ducking. Beat two: reflect one honest piece of credit back to them.

Not because you're minimizing yourself, but because you're naming reality.

It can be as simple as, "Thank you, that means a lot. Your questions helped me sharpen it," or, "I appreciate that, and your feedback last week really helped." That takes five seconds and changes the tone from spotlight to connection. You still own your work. You're just showing that good outcomes are usually a team sport.

Once this week, when praise comes your way, catch it, then add one true line about how they contributed. Keep it short and unceremonious. No speech, no theatrical modesty. Just clean acknowledgment in both directions. People remember that feeling because it's rare: they gave you something, and you let the moment include them too.

Tip 156: Use Return Paths Beyond Praise

This move isn't only for "You're amazing" moments. Any time someone brings you something positive, you can create a return path that deepens the connection. Gable's work suggests that when people share good news and you respond in an active, engaged way, they don't just feel good about the event. They feel good about you. So if they say, "My presentation actually went well," you might respond with: "That's awesome. I knew you'd bring clarity to it. What part are you proudest of?" If they say, "I finally booked that trip," you could go with: "Yes! I love that for you.

I've seen how long you've wanted that break." And when they compliment you: "You did great with that client call." "Thanks. And I really appreciated you jumping in at the right moments, it made it feel like a real team effort." Notice the pattern. You receive the positive moment, then add something that reflects them back. It stops being a solo win and starts feeling like the two of you are noticing what's good in each other.

An easy way to practice: pick one person you're close to and decide that every time something good passes between you, you'll add one extra line that honors them or the shared moment. Not a speech. Just a small acknowledgment.

Tip 157: Keep the Return Genuine

This works best when it sounds natural, not scripted. If every response feels identical, people can feel the technique instead of the warmth. Keep the shape simple, then adapt to the moment: thank them, add one true line that includes them, and move on.

Try short versions: "Thanks, that means a lot. Your prep made my part easier." Or, "I appreciate that. You set me up really well there." Keep it clean and specific. You're not performing humility. You're turning praise into shared connection without making the moment heavy.

Chapter 70: Ask: What Outcome Do We Want?

It's weird how fast your brain can downgrade someone from "person I care about" to "opponent I must defeat." One slightly sharp comment, a raised eyebrow, a misunderstood text, and suddenly your inner lawyer is sprinting down the hallway grabbing evidence and drafting closing arguments. At that point, you're not in a relationship. You're in a trial. Psychologist Igor Grossmann studies something called "wise reasoning," which is basically how people think when they're at their best instead of at their angriest. One of the patterns he's found is that when people mentally step outside the heat of the moment, they make better choices. Less ego, more perspective.

A simple way to do that in conflict is to ask yourself one question before you open your mouth: "How do I want them to feel at the end of this?" Not "How do I prove I'm right?" Not "How do I win?" Just, "What do I want their emotional state to be when we walk away?" Respected? Clear? Still close to me, even if this was hard? That answer quietly rewires your tone, your word choice, and even your timing. You stop aiming for victory and start aiming for an outcome you can live with later.

Tip 158: Let the End-State Pick Your Tone

People often charge into a tense conversation on autopilot. Whatever emotion is loudest in the moment picks the tone. You feel hurt, so you go sharp. You feel scared, so you go controlling. Later, you're stuck apologizing for the way you said it, even if the content was fair. The conflict outcome question interrupts that reflex. Before you speak, do a quick internal check: "At the end of this, I want them to feel respected, even if we disagree." "I want them to feel clear on where I stand, not confused or attacked." "I want us both to feel like we're on the same side of the problem." Once you name that, it becomes a quiet filter.

You notice when your volume, sarcasm, or word choice is about punishing them instead of reaching that end-state. You might still be firm, but you're less likely to go for the cheap shots you'll regret later. Before your next tricky talk, literally pause for three seconds and ask, "How do I want them to feel when this is done?" Pick one word. Then, as you speak, aim your tone at that word. Not perfection, just alignment. You'll still say hard things, but they'll land in a way the relationship can survive.

Tip 159: Design the Win for Both of You

A lot of conflict goes sideways because the hidden goal is, "I need to win this exchange." That goal makes your tone sharper, your listening narrower, and your closing messy. Even if you "win," the relationship takes damage on the way out.

Before the hard talk, define a better outcome: What would a good ending feel like for both of us? Maybe it's "clear and respected," not "defeated and correct." Once you name that, your language starts to change. You ask better questions. You drop fewer cheap shots. You stay firm without turning combative.

Useful lines sound like this: "I'm not trying to beat you; I want us clearer by the end." Or, "I care more about getting this right together than scoring points." Keep one sentence of desired end-state in front of you before the conversation starts, and use it as a filter. If

your next line serves that goal, say it. If it only serves
your ego, rewrite it.

Chapter 71: Recover the Social Fumble Fast

A social fumble usually arrives fast: you say something clumsy, the air shifts, and everyone feels the wobble. Maybe you interrupted, missed the tone, or joked at the wrong moment. The key move is not pretending it never happened; it's recovering cleanly before the awkwardness hardens. Psychologist June Tangney studies self-conscious emotions like shame and guilt, and one of her big findings is that how you handle your own mistakes matters more than pretending you never make any. Shame freezes and hides. Guilt notices and repairs. People respond much better when you can acknowledge a slip lightly and honestly, instead of spiraling inside your head. In conversation, that looks like, "That came out weird.

Let me try that again," or "Okay, that was clumsy, what I meant was..." A social fumble recovery line is exactly that: a quick, honest reset. You don't vanish into awkward silence, and you don't launch into a five-minute apology tour. You just flag the misstep, restate yourself, and move on. It breaks the tension for everyone, shows you're self-aware, and often makes you oddly more likable. People aren't looking for perfection. They relax around the person who can stumble, laugh at it a little, and keep the connection intact.

Tip 160: Call the Fumble, Hit Reset

Silence after a misstep is where your brain writes horror stories. "They think I'm awful." "I've ruined everything." "I can never speak again, goodbye." Meanwhile, most people would be totally fine if you just gave them a quick, clear repair. Your goal is not to erase the moment but to clean it up enough that everyone can relax. Simple, low-drama lines you can use: "That came out wrong. Let me say that better." "Wait, that wording sucked. What I meant was…" "Sorry, that was clumsy. I was trying to say…" Then you restate your point, shorter and kinder. No extra self-hate, no long monologue about how you always do this. The fix should be smaller than the thing you're fixing.

When you next feel that internal "oh no" flash after something you said, treat it as your cue for one of these lines. Literally hear the fumble, tag it out loud, and go again. You'll feel your own shoulders drop, and the other person usually softens too. You just proved you can self-correct without making them carry the awkwardness for you.

Tip 161: Use Humor and Proportion

When you fumble a sentence, the repair should match the size of the mistake. Small awkward line? Small reset. If you launch into a dramatic apology spiral, now the other person has to manage your emotions too, which is not exactly the healing vibe.

Try a light correction instead: "That came out weird, let me try again." Or, "My brain tripped over that sentence, what I meant was…" If you nicked something sensitive, add one direct acknowledgment, then restate: "Sorry, that sounded harsher than I meant. Here's what I was trying to say." Then keep moving. Don't build a memorial for one clumsy phrase.

Practice one "take two" a day in normal conversation. Not because you're broken, but because recovery is a social skill. The more you do it in real time, the less you catastrophize afterward. People rarely remember the original stumble. They remember whether you handled it with proportion, honesty, and a little grace under pressure.

Chapter 72: Soften Status Early

Some people say, "Please, call me Steve," and every other signal says, "Address me as Your Majesty." Corner office, polished sentences, everything tidy and controlled. Technically they're being friendly. Physically, you're still half in performance mode. So you give safe takes, keep your real opinions on mute, and save honesty for someone who feels less like a walking performance review. Power-distance research by Geert Hofstede suggests that in any setup where one person clearly has more status, people instinctively hold back. They censor themselves, avoid risks, and keep anything messy off the table. Amy Edmondson's work on psychological safety lines up with this.

Teams only really speak up, share ideas, or admit mistakes when the status gap feels emotionally smaller, even if nothing changed on the org chart. That's what the status softener move is trying to fix. You keep your role, your authority, your expertise. You just add one small, human detail that says, "It's safe to be a person in here." It might be, "If I shuffle these pages, it's because I spilled coffee on my notes this morning," or, "I triple-checked this, because I definitely got it wrong the first time." One tiny imperfection or offbeat detail takes you out of the marble statue category and puts you back in the human column. People stop bracing.

The conversation speeds up, loosens up, and gets closer to the truth.

Tip 162: Drop One Human Detail Early

If people are bracing around you, one tiny human detail can drop the pressure fast. You don't need a dramatic "let me bare my soul" moment. One normal, slightly imperfect line is enough to signal, "I'm a person, not a podium."

Try: "If I glance down, it's because I rewrote these notes after spilling coffee on page one." Or, "If I sound a little robotic, I practiced this in my kitchen and my kitchen was not impressed." Quick smile, then keep going.

The key is proportion. Give one real detail, then move into substance. If you overdo it, it sounds like a strategy. If you do it lightly, it reads as confidence. People stop performing for you and start talking to you.

Use this where status is in the room: manager-to-team, senior-to-junior, or even socially confident-to-new person. One honest line at the start can save ten minutes of stiffness.

Tip 163: Use Softeners for Real Talk

Being "approachable" isn't enough. People open up when they hear explicit permission. A softener line does that without sounding soft or vague.

Try something like, "I might be missing part of this, so if something feels off, say it and we'll sort it." Or, "I'm still refining this too, so push back where needed." Those lines work because they lower defensiveness on both sides. You're not pretending to be uncertain about everything. You're just telling the truth: better thinking usually comes from two brains, not one.

Then do the hard part: respond well when they actually challenge you. If you invite honesty and punish it, the door closes for months.

Use one softener line early in your next serious conversation. Keep it plain, keep it brief, and back it up with your reaction. That reaction is what people remember later, not your exact wording.

Chapter 73: Build an Easy On-Ramp

There are few things more awkward than hovering at the edge of a group conversation, waiting for a gap that never comes. They're mid-story, everyone's laughing, and you're stuck playing "Find The Opening" like it is a stealth video game. Even in one-on-one talks, plenty of people sit quietly, not because they have nothing to say, but because they're not sure when or how to jump in without derailing things. One fix lives on the host side of the interaction: build on-ramps for people. Little cues like, "If you've got a different angle, jump in," or, "Stop me if this stops making sense," show people it is okay to cut across your sentence, to add a detail, to disagree.

You're basically drawing dotted lines on the road. They no longer have to wait for a perfect silence. They know they have permission to merge. Elizabeth Stokoe, who spends her time dissecting real conversations, found that these kinds of micro-invitations lower the social cost of speaking. When people are told where they can join and reassured they will not be swatted away, they step in sooner and more honestly. A moment that used to feel like "me talking at you" starts to feel like "us building this together." And once that shift happens, even the quietest person in the circle has a much easier time bringing their real thoughts to the table.

Tip 164: Plant Easy Entry Points

A lot of people say, "Jump in anytime," then speak in five-minute monologues that make jumping in socially illegal. To get real participation, build entry points on purpose.

At the start, use a simple cue: "I'll sketch this quickly, then I want your read." Midstream, drop an on-ramp: "You've probably seen this too, right?" or "Does this match your experience or not really?" These cues tell people where they can enter without feeling rude.

One rule matters more than the wording: if someone takes the on-ramp, stop talking. Don't bulldoze over the exact participation you asked for.

Try two on-ramps in your next conversation: one early, one around the middle. Nothing fancy. You're just replacing the invisible "wait your turn forever" rule with a visible "you're welcome in now" rule. That tiny design choice changes who speaks and how quickly.

Tip 165: Use Midpoint Checkpoints

On-ramps get people into the conversation. Checkpoints keep them in once you're the one talking for longer than a minute.

While talking, drop one midpoint choice: "Short version or full version?" "Want the context first, or the bottom line?" "Should we stay here or shift to solutions?" These aren't filler lines. They hand control back before attention drops off a cliff.

Also give permission to interrupt cleanly: "If I lose you, stop me." That one line prevents the polite-nod spiral where someone has been confused for six minutes and is now emotionally gone.

In your next longer explanation, place one checkpoint around the halfway point and actually pause. Don't race through your own checkpoint. Conversations feel better when people can steer in small ways.

Chapter 74: Use a Neutral Buffer

You know the feeling when a conversation suddenly gets way too direct. It might be a performance review, a hard relationship talk, or a "we need to clear the air" moment. Eye contact starts to feel like a spotlight. Your brain is busy running threat assessments while your mouth tries to act normal. It is a lot for two faces to carry. One simple way to take the heat down a notch is to give both of you something else to look at. Developmental psychologist Michael Tomasello talks about "joint attention," the way people connect more easily when they focus on a shared object for a bit. It could be a toy, a book, a screen, a sketch.

When two people shift their gaze to the same thing, tension tends to drop and collaboration gets easier. It is like moving the emotional center of gravity off your chests and onto the table between you. That is the basic move here: bring a neutral object into the conversation and invite both sets of eyes onto it. A document, a note, a calendar, a message on your phone, even a quick doodle on a napkin. A simple "Can we look at it together?" quietly changes the frame from "me versus you" to "the two of us looking at this situation." The words might sound small, but your nervous system usually feels the difference right away.

Tip 166: Put the Problem on the Table

Hard talks go sideways when the issue feels attached to a person's identity. A fast fix is to externalize the problem so both of you can look at it, not at each other.

Pull up the email. Write the timeline. Open the shared doc. Sketch the two options on paper. Then say, "Let's look at this together." That sentence quietly shifts the frame from blame to joint analysis.

When the issue is visible, people defend less and think more. You stop arguing from memory and start reacting to the same object. That reduces misfires like "That's not what happened" vs. "Yes it was."

Use this in your next tense conversation, especially if the same fight keeps repeating. Put the issue in the middle of the table and keep both of you on the same side of it. You're not making the conversation softer; you're making it solvable.

Tip 167: Use Objects to Cool the Room

You don't need a formal worksheet to cool a tense moment. Everyday objects work fine. Menu, calendar, notes app, even the back of a receipt if that's what's there.

The aim is simple: give both sets of eyes a shared place to land. Face-to-face intensity drops, and people can think again. Try, "Can we map this quickly?" or, "Let's check dates so we're not guessing." It sounds practical because it is practical, but it also does emotional cleanup in real time.

This move is especially useful when a conversation starts feeling like a stare-down. Bring in a neutral object and turn "me versus you" into "us versus this messy thing."

You'll start seeing opportunities everywhere once you practice it. A small shared surface often does more than a perfect argument ever will in a tense moment, especially when emotions are already high.

Chapter 75: Share a Soft Parallel

There's a very specific kind of conversational crime we've all committed: someone shares a story, and fifteen seconds later it's somehow about you. They mention a hard day at work, and your brain sprints to, "That reminds me of the time I…" Now they're in the background of their own moment, and you're giving a TED Talk about your struggle. You didn't mean to hijack it. But emotionally, that's how it lands. Social psychologist Leon Festinger's work on social comparison highlighted something useful here. People feel closer to those who seem similar in experience, as long as it doesn't turn into a competition. "You too?" can be bonding.

"You think that's bad, wait till you hear my story" kills the mood instantly. The trick is to use your experience as a bridge, not a spotlight. That's what the soft parallel share does. Instead of dropping a full "Now it's my turn" monologue, you offer a tiny, non-competing echo like, "I had a small moment like that last week. Not the same, but similar in feel." One short line, maybe a quick snapshot, then you hand it right back to them. It says, "You're not alone," without stealing the scene. Done well, it feels warm, relatable, and quietly charming.

Tip 168: Keep Your Story Smaller

Parallel sharing works only if your story stays smaller than theirs. If they share stress and you respond with your life epic, the focus flips and trust thins out.

Use a quick frame: "Not the same, but I had a smaller version of that." Then keep it short, one scene max. Think two sentences, not a mini memoir. Your job is to signal recognition, not seize the mic.

A good internal check is: am I joining or topping? Joining sounds like, "I get that feeling." Topping sounds like, "Wait till you hear mine." You already know which one leaves people feeling seen.

When someone opens up, offer a small parallel and then return to them quickly. This isn't about proving you've suffered too. It's about making their moment feel less lonely, more understood, and easier to keep talking about.

Tip 169: Use a Parallel, Then Return to Center

A soft parallel share should behave like a bridge, not a road trip. You step onto it briefly, then bring the conversation back to them.

Simple sequence:

5. Small parallel: "Not the same, but I had a lighter version of that."
6. One feeling line: "It rattled me more than I expected."
7. Return question: "What part hit you hardest?"

That final step is where most people miss. They share, then keep going, and suddenly the spotlight moved. If you ask a clean follow-up, the other person feels accompanied, not replaced.

Run this today in one real conversation. Keep your parallel to two or three lines max, then hand it back with a question that invites depth. When done right, people feel two things at once: "You get it," and

"You're still here with me." That combination is rare and incredibly memorable.

Tip 170: Repair Fast If You Took Over

Sometimes you notice too late that your "same here" moment quietly became a takeover. Don't panic. Repair it in one line and hand it back.

Try: "I just made that about me for a second. Bring me back to your part." Or: "I sidetracked us. What was the part that hit you hardest?" Quick ownership, clean return.

This works because it shows self-awareness without drama. You're not launching into an apology speech. You're re-centering them fast enough that the original emotional thread stays alive.

Run this once the next time you catch yourself over-talking after a parallel. Done well, people feel respected, not replaced.

Chapter 76: Offer Two Options

Open-ended questions sound wise in theory. "So… how did that make you feel?" "What was that like for you?" In reality, you can almost see people's brains freeze. They stare at the ceiling like the answer is hidden in the light fixture. It's not that they have nothing to say. It's that you just handed them a blank canvas and no brushes. Give a stressed brain infinite options and it spins like a browser with forty tabs and 2% battery. Psychologist Amos Tversky, who spent his life studying how people make decisions, kept finding the same thing: we think faster and more clearly when choices are narrowed. Give someone twenty options and they stall. Give them two and they move.

The same rules apply in conversation. Instead of tossing out huge, vague questions, you can offer a tiny fork in the road: "Did it feel more exciting or more overwhelming?" "Was it more about the timing or the pressure?" Suddenly their brain has something to push against. That's the paired-option prompt. You give them two simple possibilities and let them react. Maybe they pick one. Maybe they say, "Honestly, it was both." Maybe they say, "Actually, it was neither, it was this other thing." Perfect. Either way, you just made it easier for them to step into the conversation instead of staring into question void. You lowered the cognitive load, which makes everything feel more relaxed and more real.

Tip 171: Offer Two Words to Start

Open-ended questions are useful, but in emotional moments they can feel like homework. Giving two options helps people start talking without feeling examined.

Instead of "How was it?" try "More draining or more relieving?" Instead of "What happened?" try "Was it the content that bothered you, or the tone?" You're not forcing a binary forever. You're offering a launch point.

Once they choose, you can expand: "Say more about that." The two-word frame lowers cognitive load, especially when someone is stressed, tired, or trying to make sense of mixed feelings in real time.

Use this lightly. If every line sounds like a personality quiz, it gets weird fast. But one well-placed two-option prompt can turn vague answers into clear ones and make the other person feel helped, not interrogated. Think nudge, not script. Keep it conversational and human, and adjust based on their tone.

Tip 172: Use Pairs as Launchpads

Paired options are just a starting ramp. The useful part is what happens after they answer. You're not giving them a test, you're giving them something easier than "So… how was it?" so their brain has somewhere to land. Once they pick one (or reject both), that's your cue to zoom in. A quick example: "Did it feel more exciting or more overwhelming?" If they say "overwhelming," follow with, "Overwhelming in what way?" Then keep following their wording. If neither option fits, leave the door open: "Or neither of those; how would you describe it?" That keeps people from feeling trapped in your menu and naturally moves the conversation deeper. Try this lightly.

One good A-or-B prompt plus one precise follow-up usually beats a long chain of prompts.

Chapter 77: Match Turn Length

There's a special kind of awkward when two people talk in totally different "sizes." One person answers in full paragraphs with footnotes and backstory. The other responds in tiny word-bites like "Yeah," "Totally," and "That's cool." Nobody's wrong, but it feels like trying to play catch with someone who keeps tossing a pebble after you've lobbed a bowling ball. The rhythm just never quite settles. Conversation analyst Stephen Levinson and others have studied how we trade speaking turns. It's not just when we speak that matters, but how long we hold the floor. When one person consistently drops long monologues while the other offers quick fragments, it creates this low-level friction.

The talkative one may feel like they're dragging the whole interaction. The quieter one can start feeling steamrolled or unimportant. Neither is having much fun. Think of the turn-length harmonizer as a little volume knob for how much you say at once. Instead of defaulting to your usual length, you glance at how much they're sharing and aim for a similar chunk size. If they tend to answer in two or three sentences, you stay roughly in that range. If they unpack things in longer stretches, you let yourself do the same. It stops feeling like two different conversation styles colliding and starts feeling more like walking in step with someone, where the strides aren't identical but the pace matches.

Tip 173: Match Reply Length, Not Personality

You're not becoming a different person to do this. You're just noticing how much space they naturally take, then aiming for the same neighborhood. Some people speak in one-sentence snapshots; others need a short arc before they land. If you tend to ramble and they're crisp, tighten to two or three contained sentences. If you're usually very brief and they're more expansive, add one extra line of context before handing it back. You can test this quickly. In your next conversation, pick a rough sentence count based on their default and aim near that number for a few turns. Don't obsess.

Use it as a loose rhythm guide so the exchange stops feeling like one person is carrying all the weight while the other drops drive-by replies.

Tip 174: Use Turn Length to Make Room

Turn-length harmonizing does more than keep you from rambling. It also quietly teaches people how much space they're allowed to take. When you give full, thoughtful answers instead of clipped ones, you're sending a message: it's okay to stretch out a bit with me. You can reinforce that with a couple of small habits. If they give a very short answer, don't rush to fill the silence. Leave a tiny pause and keep your attention on them; a lot of people will naturally keep going once they sense you're still listening. When you do ask follow-ups, match your question to their style.

With someone who usually speaks in headlines, you might say, "Do you want to say a bit more about that, or does that pretty much cover it?" With a natural talker, you can gently set the frame: "Should I get the short version or the full download?" It comes down to choice. You're making it clear there's no penalty for talking longer, and no pressure if they'd rather keep it tight. If there's someone in your life who often seems rushed or talked over, try paying attention to how

long they normally let themselves talk and adjust to
that range.

Chapter 78: Run the 30-Day Integration Loop

Reading tips is useful. Running reps is what changes your relationships.

If you want this book to become behavior instead of trivia, run a simple 30-day loop:

8. Days 1-7: Pick one tip per day and run it in a low-stakes conversation.
9. Days 8-14: Keep one tip from week one, then add one new tip per day.
10. Days 15-21: Use your reps in one medium-stakes conversation each day.
11. Days 22-30: Keep only the tips that feel natural and get clear results.

Use one tiny daily log:

12. Tip used.
13. Situation.
14. What changed.
15. What to tweak tomorrow.

No essay. One minute is enough.

After 30 days, start a maintenance loop so this sticks:

16. Pick three core tips as your non-negotiables.
17. Run one deliberate rep each week in a real conversation.
18. Do a weekly check-in: where did I connect well, where did I rush, what will I test next?
19. Every month, swap in one new tip and retire one that doesn't fit your style.

This keeps your social skill set alive without turning your life into a training camp.

If you get off track, nothing broke. Restart with one tip, one person, one conversation. That's always enough to get momentum back.

Good social skill is not about being impressive in one perfect interaction. It's about being reliably easier to talk to over time.

That's the real finish line: people feel better after talking with you than they did before.

Conclusion: Keep the Science, Keep the Door Open

If you made it this far, you've already done something uncommon: you paid attention to how conversations actually work.

Not in a polished quote-card way. In real life. In the awkward pauses, clunky recoveries, half-finished thoughts, and those tiny moments where someone decides whether to open up or pull back.

That matters more than most people realize.

A lot of people spend years trying to sound smarter, smoother, more impressive. But better conversations usually come from better moves, not better performance. A pause instead of a rush. A follow-up instead of a monologue. A reset instead of a spiral. A handoff instead of a hijack.

That's the science of charisma in everyday life.

Not a personality costume. Not charm-the-room theater. Just repeatable social choices that help people feel safe, seen, and interested.

From the outside, these moves can look tiny. Over time, they change everything.

Connection is rarely one big movie moment. It's a bunch of small moments handled well, over and over. That's how trust gets built. That's how people start to relax around you.

So keep the system simple:

1. Pick one move.
2. Use it today.
3. Notice what changed.
4. Keep what works.

That's the job.

You don't need to become a different person. You don't need to be "on" all the time. You don't need to turn every conversation into a deep emotional summit. You just need enough awareness to notice what's happening and enough steadiness to respond in a way that helps.

Some days you'll do this really well. Some days you'll interrupt, over-explain, miss the cue, or read the room wrong. Fine. That's reps. Own it, repair it, keep moving.

If this book lands the way it's meant to, your life won't become nonstop profound dialogue. It'll become something better: fewer awkward collisions, more ease, cleaner repairs, clearer asks, warmer exits, and more people feeling like they can be real with you.

And maybe the biggest shift is this: you stop trying to win conversations, and start trying to build them.

That's where better friendships come from. Better teamwork. Better dating. Better leadership. Better family dynamics. Not because you became someone else, but because you practiced the science until it felt like your natural way of showing up.

Endnotes

1. Thomas Gilovich, Victoria Husted Medvec, and Kenneth Savitsky, "The Spotlight Effect in Social Judgment: An Egocentric Bias in Estimates of the Salience of One's Own Actions and Appearance," *Journal of Personality and Social Psychology* 78, no. 2 (2000): 211-222.
2. Tanya L. Chartrand and John A. Bargh, "The Chameleon Effect: The Perception-Behavior Link and Social Interaction," *Journal of Personality and Social Psychology* 76, no. 6 (1999): 893-910.
3. Jon Jecker and David Landy, "Liking a Person as a Function of Doing Him a Favor," *Human Relations* 22, no. 4 (1969): 371-378.
4. Alex Pentland, *Honest Signals: How They Shape Our World* (Cambridge, MA: MIT Press, 2008).
5. Erica J. Boothby and Vanessa K. Bohns, "Why a Simple Act of Kindness Is Not as Simple as It Seems: Underestimating the Positive Impact of Compliments," *Journal of Personality and Social Psychology* 121, no. 6 (2021): 1142-1164.
6. Elliot Aronson, Ben Willerman, and Joanne Floyd, "The Effect of a Pratfall on Increasing Interpersonal Attractiveness," *Psychonomic Science* 4, no. 6 (1966): 227-228.
7. Harvey Sacks, Emanuel A. Schegloff, and Gail Jefferson, "A Simplest Systematics for the Organization of Turn-Taking for Conversation," *Language* 50, no. 4 (1974): 696-735.
8. Neville Moray, "Attention in Dichotic Listening: Affective Cues and the Influence of Instructions," *Quarterly Journal of Experimental Psychology* 11, no. 1 (1959): 56-60; Nancy Wood and Nelson Cowan, "The Cocktail Party Phenomenon Revisited: How Frequent Are Attention Shifts to

One's Name in an Irrelevant Auditory Channel?" *Journal of Experimental Psychology: Learning, Memory, and Cognition* 21, no. 1 (1995): 255-260.

9. Elizabeth Couper-Kuhlen, *English Speech Rhythm: Form and Function in Everyday Verbal Interaction* (Amsterdam: John Benjamins, 1993).

10. Alison Wood Brooks, Karen Huang, Michael S. Yeomans, Julia Minson, and Francesca Gino, "It Doesn't Hurt to Ask: Question-Asking Increases Liking," *Journal of Personality and Social Psychology* 113, no. 3 (2017): 430-452.

11. Melanie C. Green and Timothy C. Brock, "The Role of Transportation in the Persuasiveness of Public Narratives," *Journal of Personality and Social Psychology* 79, no. 5 (2000): 701-721.

12. Arthur Aron, Elaine N. Aron, Norman D. Melinat, Robert D. Vallone, and Renee J. Bator, "The Experimental Generation of Interpersonal Closeness: A Procedure and Some Preliminary Findings," *Personality and Social Psychology Bulletin* 23, no. 4 (1997): 363-377.

13. William R. Miller and Stephen Rollnick, *Motivational Interviewing: Helping People Change*, 3rd ed. (New York: Guilford Press, 2013).

14. Daniel Kahneman, Barbara L. Fredrickson, Charles A. Schreiber, and Donald A. Redelmeier, "When More Pain Is Preferred to Less: Adding a Better End," *Psychological Science* 4, no. 6 (1993): 401-405.

15. Graham D. Bodie, "The Active-Empathic Listening Scale (AELS): Conceptualization and Evidence of Validity Within the Interpersonal Domain," *Communication Quarterly* 59, no. 3 (2011): 277-295.

16. Carl R. Rogers and Richard E. Farson, "Active Listening," in *Communicating in Business Today*,

ed. R. G. Newman, M. A. Danzinger, and M. Cohen (Washington, DC: Heath and Company, 1987).

17. Alison Wood Brooks, Karen Huang, Michael S. Yeomans, Julia Minson, and Francesca Gino, "It Doesn't Hurt to Ask: Question-Asking Increases Liking," *Journal of Personality and Social Psychology* 113, no. 3 (2017): 430-452.

18. Matthew D. Lieberman, Naomi I. Eisenberger, Molly J. Crockett, S. Matthew Tom, Jennifer H. Pfeifer, and Baldwin M. Way, "Putting Feelings into Words: Affect Labeling Disrupts Amygdala Activity in Response to Affective Stimuli," *Psychological Science* 18, no. 5 (2007): 421-428.

19. Alvin W. Gouldner, "The Norm of Reciprocity: A Preliminary Statement," *American Sociological Review* 25, no. 2 (1960): 161-178.

20. Norbert Schwarz, "Metacognitive Experiences in Consumer Judgment and Decision Making," *Journal of Consumer Psychology* 14, no. 4 (2004): 332-348.

21. Edward T. Hall, *The Hidden Dimension* (Garden City, NY: Doubleday, 1966).

22. Emanuel A. Schegloff, *Sequence Organization in Interaction: A Primer in Conversation Analysis* (Cambridge: Cambridge University Press, 2007).

23. Alexander Todorov, Anesu N. Mandisodza, Amir Goren, and Crystal C. Hall, "Inferences of Competence from Faces Predict Election Outcomes," *Science* 308, no. 5728 (2005): 1623-1626.

24. Edward L. Deci and Richard M. Ryan, "The 'What' and 'Why' of Goal Pursuits: Human Needs and the Self-Determination of Behavior," *Psychological Inquiry* 11, no. 4 (2000): 227-268.

25. Virginia P. Richmond, James C. McCroskey, and Amy M. Johnson, "Development of the Nonverbal Immediacy Scale (NIS): Measures of Self- and

Other-Perceived Nonverbal Immediacy," *Communication Quarterly* 51, no. 4 (2003): 504-517.

26. Roger Fisher, William Ury, and Bruce Patton, *Getting to Yes: Negotiating Agreement Without Giving In*, 3rd ed. (New York: Penguin, 2011).

27. John M. Gottman, *The Marriage Clinic: A Scientifically Based Marital Therapy* (New York: Norton, 1999).

28. James J. Gross, "The Emerging Field of Emotion Regulation: An Integrative Review," *Review of General Psychology* 2, no. 3 (1998): 271-299.

29. Robert A. Emmons and Michael E. McCullough, "Counting Blessings Versus Burdens: An Experimental Investigation of Gratitude and Subjective Well-Being in Daily Life," *Journal of Personality and Social Psychology* 84, no. 2 (2003): 377-389.

30. John A. Bargh, Mark Chen, and Lara Burrows, "Automaticity of Social Behavior: Direct Effects of Trait Construct and Stereotype Activation on Action," *Journal of Personality and Social Psychology* 71, no. 2 (1996): 230-244.

31. Diana I. Tamir and Jason P. Mitchell, "Disclosing Information About the Self Is Intrinsically Rewarding," *Proceedings of the National Academy of Sciences* 109, no. 21 (2012): 8038-8043.

32. Nancy L. Collins and Lynn C. Miller, "Self-Disclosure and Liking: A Meta-Analytic Review," *Psychological Bulletin* 116, no. 3 (1994): 457-475.

33. Marc A. Brackett, Susan E. Rivers, and Peter Salovey, "Emotional Intelligence: Implications for Personal, Social, Academic, and Workplace Success," *Social and Personality Psychology Compass* 5, no. 1 (2011): 88-103.

34. Elaine Hatfield, John T. Cacioppo, and Richard L. Rapson, *Emotional Contagion* (Cambridge:

Cambridge University Press, 1994); Robert W. Levenson and John M. Gottman, "Marital Interaction: Physiological Linkage and Affective Exchange," *Journal of Personality and Social Psychology* 45, no. 3 (1983): 587-597.

35. Shelley E. Taylor and Susan T. Fiske, "Point of View and Perceptions of Causality," *Journal of Personality and Social Psychology* 32, no. 3 (1975): 439-445.

36. Robert Rosenthal and Lenore Jacobson, *Pygmalion in the Classroom* (New York: Holt, Rinehart and Winston, 1968).

37. Harry T. Reis, "Perceived Partner Responsiveness as an Organizing Construct in the Study of Intimacy and Closeness," in *Handbook of Closeness and Intimacy*, ed. Dan P. McAdams and Eli J. Finkel (Mahwah, NJ: Lawrence Erlbaum, 2004), 201-225.

38. Todd B. Kashdan, Patrick E. McKnight, and John C. Fincham, "When Curiosity Breeds Intimacy: Taking Advantage of Intimacy Opportunities and Transforming Boring Conversations," *Journal of Personality* 79, no. 6 (2011): 1369-1402.

39. Jerome Bruner, "The Narrative Construction of Reality," *Critical Inquiry* 18, no. 1 (1991): 1-21.

40. Daniel M. Oppenheimer, "Consequences of Erudite Vernacular Utilized Irrespective of Necessity: Problems with Using Long Words Needlessly," *Applied Cognitive Psychology* 20, no. 2 (2006): 139-156.

41. Barbara L. Fredrickson, "The Role of Positive Emotions in Positive Psychology: The Broaden-and-Build Theory of Positive Emotions," *American Psychologist* 56, no. 3 (2001): 218-226.

42. H. Paul Grice, "Logic and Conversation," in *Syntax and Semantics, Vol. 3: Speech Acts*, ed. Peter Cole and Jerry L. Morgan (New York: Academic Press, 1975), 41-58.

43. Donn Byrne, *The Attraction Paradigm* (New York: Academic Press, 1971).

44. Dan P. McAdams, *The Stories We Live By: Personal Myths and the Making of the Self* (New York: Guilford Press, 1993).

45. Carol S. Dweck and Claudia M. Mueller, "Praise for Intelligence Can Undermine Children's Motivation and Performance," *Journal of Personality and Social Psychology* 75, no. 1 (1998): 33-52.

46. Erving Goffman, *Frame Analysis: An Essay on the Organization of Experience* (Cambridge, MA: Harvard University Press, 1974).

47. Christopher Peterson and Martin E. P. Seligman, *Character Strengths and Virtues: A Handbook and Classification* (New York: Oxford University Press, 2004).

48. John P. Caughlin, "Family Communication Standards and Topic Avoidance," *Human Communication Research* 29, no. 4 (2003): 532-562; Laura K. Guerrero, Peter A. Andersen, and Walid A. Afifi, *Close Encounters: Communication in Relationships*, 4th ed. (Los Angeles: SAGE, 2011).

49. Elizabeth Stokoe, *Talk: The Science of Conversation and the Art of Being Ourselves* (New York: Viking, 2018).

50. Martin A. Conway and Christopher W. Pleydell-Pearce, "The Construction of Autobiographical Memories in the Self-Memory System," *Psychological Review* 107, no. 2 (2000): 261-288; Robyn Fivush, "The Development of Autobiographical Memory," *Annual Review of Psychology* 62 (2011): 559-582.

51. Dacher Keltner and Jonathan Haidt, "Approaching Awe, a Moral, Spiritual, and Aesthetic Emotion," *Cognition and Emotion* 17, no. 2 (2003): 297-314.

52. John M. Gottman and Nan Silver, *The Seven Principles for Making Marriage Work* (New York: Crown, 1999).

53. Shalom H. Schwartz, "Universals in the Content and Structure of Values: Theoretical Advances and Empirical Tests in 20 Countries," *Advances in Experimental Social Psychology* 25 (1992): 1-65.

54. Rachel A. Simmons, Peter C. Gordon, and Dianne L. Chambless, "Pronouns in Marital Interaction: What Do 'You' and 'I' Say About Marital Health?" *Psychological Science* 16, no. 12 (2005): 932-936; Susan T. Fiske, Amy J. C. Cuddy, and Peter Glick, "Universal Dimensions of Social Cognition: Warmth and Competence," *Trends in Cognitive Sciences* 11, no. 2 (2007): 77-83.

55. Herbert H. Clark, *Using Language* (Cambridge: Cambridge University Press, 1996).

56. Harvey Sacks, *Lectures on Conversation*, ed. Gail Jefferson (Oxford: Blackwell, 1992); Emanuel A. Schegloff, *Sequence Organization in Interaction: A Primer in Conversation Analysis* (Cambridge: Cambridge University Press, 2007).

57. Susan T. Fiske and Steven L. Neuberg, "A Continuum of Impression Formation, from Category-Based to Individuating Processes," in *Advances in Experimental Social Psychology*, vol. 23, ed. Mark P. Zanna (San Diego: Academic Press, 1990), 1-74; Joseph Berger, M. Hamit Fisek, Robert Z. Norman, and Morris Zelditch Jr., *Status Characteristics and Social Interaction* (New York: Elsevier, 1977).

58. Tania Singer, Ben Seymour, John O'Doherty, Holger Kaube, Raymond J. Dolan, and Chris D. Frith, "Empathy for Pain Involves the Affective but Not Sensory Components of Pain," *Science* 303, no. 5661 (2004): 1157-1162.

59. Elizabeth J. Krumrei-Mancuso and Steven V. Rouse, "The Development and Validation of the Comprehensive Intellectual Humility Scale," *Journal of Personality Assessment* 98, no. 2 (2016): 209-221.

60. Edward L. Deci and Richard M. Ryan, "The 'What' and 'Why' of Goal Pursuits: Human Needs and the Self-Determination of Behavior," *Psychological Inquiry* 11, no. 4 (2000): 227-268; Erika A. Patall, Harris Cooper, and Jorgianne Civey Robinson, "The Effects of Choice on Intrinsic Motivation and Related Outcomes: A Meta-Analysis of Research Findings," *Psychological Bulletin* 134, no. 2 (2008): 270-300.

61. Niall Bolger, Adam Zuckerman, and Ronald C. Kessler, "Invisible Support and Adjustment to Stress," *Journal of Personality and Social Psychology* 79, no. 6 (2000): 953-961; Vanessa K. Bohns and Frank J. Flynn, "Why Didn't You Just Ask? Underestimating the Discomfort of Help-Seeking," *Journal of Experimental Social Psychology* 46, no. 2 (2010): 402-409.

62. Shelly L. Gable, Harry T. Reis, Emily A. Impett, and Evan R. Asher, "What Do You Do When Things Go Right? The Intrapersonal and Interpersonal Benefits of Sharing Positive Events," *Journal of Personality and Social Psychology* 87, no. 2 (2004): 228-245.

63. Igor Grossmann and Ethan Kross, "Exploring Solomon's Paradox: Self-Distancing Eliminates the Self-Other Asymmetry in Wise Reasoning About Close Relationships in Younger and Older Adults," *Psychological Science* 25, no. 8 (2014): 1571-1580.

64. June Price Tangney, Jeff Stuewig, and Debra J. Mashek, "Moral Emotions and Moral Behavior," *Annual Review of Psychology* 58 (2007): 345-372.

65. Geert Hofstede, *Culture's Consequences: Comparing Values, Behaviors, Institutions and Organizations Across Nations*, 2nd ed. (Thousand Oaks, CA: Sage, 2001).

66. Amy C. Edmondson, "Psychological Safety and Learning Behavior in Work Teams," *Administrative Science Quarterly* 44, no. 2 (1999): 350-383.

67. Elizabeth Stokoe, *Talk: The Science of Conversation and the Art of Being Ourselves* (New York: Viking, 2018).

68. Malinda Carpenter, Katherine Nagell, and Michael Tomasello, "Social Cognition, Joint Attention, and Communicative Competence From 9 to 15 Months of Age," *Monographs of the Society for Research in Child Development* 63, no. 4 (1998): i-174.

69. Leon Festinger, "A Theory of Social Comparison Processes," *Human Relations* 7, no. 2 (1954): 117-140.

70. Amos Tversky and Daniel Kahneman, "Judgment Under Uncertainty: Heuristics and Biases," *Science* 185, no. 4157 (1974): 1124-1131; Sheena S. Iyengar and Mark R. Lepper, "When Choice Is Demotivating: Can One Desire Too Much of a Good Thing?" *Journal of Personality and Social Psychology* 79, no. 6 (2000): 995-1006.

71. Stephen C. Levinson and Francisco Torreira, "Timing in Turn-Taking and Its Implications for Processing Models of Language," *Frontiers in Psychology* 6 (2015): 731.